Organised Chaos

Turbocharge your ADHD superpowers

N.M. Lennon-Barrett

SUPERPOWER MASTERY

Organised Chaos: Turbocharge your ADHD Superpowers

This book is a work of nonfiction. It reflects the personal views, lived experiences, and interpretations of the author. While every effort has been made to ensure accuracy and clarity, the content is intended for informational and reflective purposes only. Readers are encouraged to use their own judgment and discretion when applying any ideas, strategies, or suggestions presented herein.

The author accepts no liability for any outcomes resulting from the use or misuse of the material in this book. Implementation is entirely at the reader's own risk.

Brand names and trademarks mentioned remain the property of their respective owners. Inclusion does not imply endorsement or affiliation.

For permissions or enquiries, contact: www.superpowermastery.com

Thank you for respecting the work, words, and weirdness that went into this creation.

To everyone living with ADHD:

You are not broken. You are brilliant.
Your chaos is not a flaw. It's a superpower.
Keep creating, questioning, and showing up as you are.
You're not alone, and you've always been enough.

Chapter 1

The Introduction

Yesterday, I was diagnosed with Autism Spectrum Disorder.

Why am I telling you that when this book is about Attention Deficit Hyperactivity Disorder? Because ... that news yesterday gave me the kick up the backside I needed, after procrastinating about writing this book for two years. The irony is that in that time I've published half a dozen books, but they are all fiction, so fuel my overactive imagination with a plethora of dopamine. This is my first non-fiction book and, as I'm my own worst critic, the procrastination monster has been doing its job.

The aim of this book is to enable you to develop your ADHD superpowers which will turbo-charge your career, life or whatever is important to you. I want you to come away from reading this book feeling better about yourself, and being able to take action that has an impact. This is not another thought leadership book which spends eons talking about a single seven-point model for eighty thousand words. I have a very low boredom threshold, so you'll be seeing none of that here. Of course, I have models, or cheat codes, as I call them, but there is more than one, so you can pick what works best for you and not be beholden to a single golden chalice. And, I promise, a shorter word count.

Right now, I am sitting in a chain coffee shop on a Saturday morning with my latte and sausage bap and tapping away at this keyboard, trying not to be distracted by the two women across from me who are airing their dirty linen in public. Apparently, Paul had it coming. From what I can pick up, he's also done it before. My overactive imagination has him cheating on someone and, of course, it's mixed up with a mob boss, because it would be boring otherwise. Paul is now in a full body cast at the local hospital, regretting his life choices. I don't know if my assumptions about Paul are true. They've moved on to one of the kids needing some expensive trainers. I zoned out because that's less interesting, and also, *how* much for kids' trainers?

This book is about the realities of navigating the workplace, and life in general, with ADHD. I was diagnosed formally in 2020. It was in the middle of the pandemic, so it was done over a Skype call, which seemed bizarre at the time. The doctor completing the assessment said he didn't need to ask me the question about whether I speak too much. I was both shocked and impressed with the quick wit and, to be fair, he wasn't wrong. I apologise in advance for the random tangents I will veer off into throughout this book, but then at least you know it is authentically me.

My ASD diagnosis, yesterday, was over Teams. In contrast, it would have felt strange if I'd been asked to attend in person. The world has not just moved on with technology, but how we look at neurodivergent people. As more people are open about living with ADHD, the social stigma diminishes, but the day-to-day barriers and challenges remain.

Before we go any further, I better introduce myself properly. Hello, I'm Nick Lennon-Barrett: husband, cat dad, author, learning geek and ADHD superhero.

What do I mean by that? For me, I regard my ADHD as a superpower, rather than a disability. Yes, there are barriers, and they can debilitate at times, but by focusing on what you can control over what you can't you can achieve your goals, dreams and maybe even tick everything off your never-ending to-do list - okay, that would be amazing, but I'm not a magician. There are limitations to these superpowers, and one of them is that the to-do list is never completely done. Sorry, but you'll need to accept that reality now. Your life will be far less stressful if you do.

A bit about my background. I was born to a teenage mother and grew up on a council estate in the north of England. Life was a challenge. I never went without food, or warmth, but the latest toy, new clothes, holidays and anything else deemed a 'luxury' was something the other kids had. The one thing I never doubted was that I was loved. I knew of people who never wanted for anything materialistic growing up, but affection was in short supply. I count myself as one of the lucky ones.

My ADHD was not formally diagnosed until I was in my early forties. Throughout my childhood and early adulthood, words like 'naughty' or 'defective' were commonly used. The challenge of not being able to regulate my emotions resulted in me having legendary temper tantrums. One was so big, I was kicked out of the family home at sixteen. It involved me smashing a window, so it was pretty epic, even by soap opera standards. It was one of those 'go big or go home' moments, or in this case, 'go big and get out of the home!'

Do I resent my mother for kicking me out? Absolutely not. I was an absolute brat and would have done the same in her shoes. And to be fair, when I came back that night having arranged a flat to move into, she begged me to stay. I was resourceful even at that age, and I knew our relationship would be stronger if we weren't in each other's pockets all the time. Things did significantly improve between us when we were no longer in the same house. I suspect she probably had undiagnosed ADHD herself. We could push each other's buttons in a way nobody else had ever done, although my husband likes to try when he's bored. To be fair, he has a relatively high success rate.

Now, I'm an award-winning learning leader, having worked across multiple organisations, including those on the FTSE 100. I've developed people from interns to CEOs across the world, in various sectors from retail to financial services. I have a master's degree in Human Resource Management, I am an accredited executive coach, and I am certified in many psychometric tools, such as Myers-Briggs, Hogan, DISC and EQ-I.

This book brings together both my knowledge and skills gained in a career of more than twenty years, and my hands-on experience of navigating the working world as someone with ADHD. It is a mix of memoir, personal development and storytelling.

This book is not just for people living with ADHD. Nobody's brain works perfectly. It's what makes us uniquely human, and not robots. We have six executive functions of the brain, and there will be at least one which every person struggles with. Perfection does not exist. That's my first big statement, but it's true. Someone's perfection will be another person's first draft.

We'll start this book by setting the scene before we get into the meat of each superpower, and how you can develop them. Finally, we'll look at how to build your own hero story, so you finish this book ready to take action.

At the end of most chapters, there will be an action for you to take away. You don't need to do them all, and I would suggest you don't. Pick a maximum of three and focus on them before tackling any others. I repeat this again for my fellow ADHDers – pick ONLY three! I see you, and know what you're thinking!

We start this journey with my origin story. What was the moment when I realised something needed to change? That would be over a decade ago, around the time my life imploded.

Chapter 2

The Origin Story

Every hero needs an origin story. The spider bite, the particle accelerator explosion and so on. As already mentioned, I wasn't formally diagnosed with ADHD until 2020, but it was almost a decade earlier when I realised not only was my brain a bit 'quirky' as is the polite term used by some, but I had superpowers. I quickly understood that if I could develop these superpowers and enhance them further, I'd be able to achieve my goals, not just in my career, but in life.

Chaotic Snowball

Before we get into the trigger event, as we'll refer to it, let me set the context for you. Two months before this 'event' happened, I had quit my steady, yet uninspiring, job without having another one to go to. It was scary to make such a bold decision when I had no savings, but I knew it was the right one for me. Two days later, my mother died suddenly. Did I retract my resignation? Of course not. I'd decided, and I was far too stubborn to back down from it.

Fast forward to the 'day of reckoning,' and I was forty-eight hours into my new job. It was the end of the day, and my boss grabbed her bag and ran out of the office without saying a word. I thought nothing of it. People have emergencies and it wasn't my business. That was until the CEO walked into the room and made it everyone's business. He informed the entire team that my boss and her boss had been suspended pending an investigation. My inside voice was clear in its summation of the situation to myself: 'Nick, WTF have you done?'

A barrage of emotions: fear, anger, confusion, and even intrigue hit me. Ask any Human Resources professional and they'll tell you that gossip is our catnip; we can't get enough of it. My intuition was telling me to run for the hills, but I was living payday to payday back then. I'd needed to borrow money to pay for my mother's funeral, which I still owed. Her first birthday since she'd died was coming up, which is on Christmas Day. Even without an ADHD diagnosis, I was self-aware enough to know that any decision I made in that moment wouldn't be logical. So, I stayed, not realising I was about to live through one of the most stressful years of my life.

In the new year, everything went back to normal. The bosses returned, and it was never spoken about. HR professionals are like bloodhounds for sniffing out gossip, but this was locked down tight. There were rumours, but nothing concrete was ever confirmed. For the next couple of months, I just wanted to keep my head above water. I needed to prove myself in the new role in order to pass probation and I had a new relationship blooming with the guy who would become my husband, although I didn't know that yet – sorry, spoilers!

I was trying to keep everything perfectly balanced, but inside I was a mess. It had been six months since my mother had died and I knew I hadn't processed the emotional impact of it. As the older sibling, I'd taken care of all the practical things, which is my forte. I am hyper-organised, obsessively so at times, but nobody ever complains in work or out, because they know stuff gets done. I was effectively running on empty. The tank was dry, and I was pushing myself as much as I could, and operating at my default stance of a hundred miles an hour, even though it felt like I was wading through treacle.

Looking back now, with the knowledge of an ADHD diagnosis, I know my emotions were dysregulated, and I was suffering from major rejection sensitivity. My mother had left me. She was the one person who I believed would always have my back, and would drive me insane at times, but was always proud of me no matter how insignificant the achievement. I think she was the only person who thought an E in Geography was something to be proud of. 'It's better than an F,' was her response – a philosophy and mindset I've tried to adopt throughout my life. Of course, my mother didn't choose to leave me or any of my siblings, but I lost my dad when I was sixteen, which was a sudden death as well. I was now a thirty-three-year-old grown man, but felt like an orphan. For the first time in over a decade, things got too much. I struggled to even breathe when trying to process my emotions, and I crashed - hard.

Phoenix Rising

My GP took one look at me and signed me off work for a month. After a week of sitting at home trying to function, I knew I was not in the best environment for my recovery. Friends and family all meant well, but this was a time I needed to be by myself. My budding relationship had imploded, which was just another stress on top of everything which had happened. Now, because of spoilers earlier, we know how things work out, but imagine all that happening at once. I was advised to go away somewhere and cut myself off, so that's what I did.

When I looked up holiday options, I had three criteria: it needed to be cheap, all-inclusive (so I didn't have to leave the hotel), and the room needed a DVD player, so I could escape into another world when needed. This was a time before iPads and streaming services. Lanzarote was the choice. I had been there once before, and did not know the place would one day feel like a second home. Little did I know but I had booked a hotel which catered to triathletes who stayed when training. I was the only person at the buffet who ate the chips and, to be fair, I do like a salad, so it wasn't all bad. Meat, salad and chips for the week was something I could work with.

As soon as I walked into my hotel room and closed the door my legs gave way, like they'd been waiting for that moment. I had to crawl across the floor and climb on to the bed, because my legs wouldn't stop shaking. Everything I'd bottled up for the past six months came out and I did something I never had before: I cried myself to sleep.

The next day, my brain was saying, 'Right, let's make plans to take over the world,' but my body was like, 'I don't think so, mister.' It was worn out, both physically and mentally. The first thing I needed was fuel. I'm a big foodie and had no recollection of ever missing dinner unless I was sick. Then it hit me; I was seriously sick, and I'd come here to start the healing process. I would not be completely renewed in a week, but I had so many things going on in my head, all competing for pole position. I needed to prioritise. How did I do that? My approach up to that point in life had been to take on anything and everything and just get it done. It had been that way since I had left home at sixteen. In a moment of clarity, I realised I needed to do something urgently – I needed to go shopping!

I came back to the hotel with notebooks, pens, and ice cream Mars Bars; it will all make sense shortly.

This all happened after breakfast, of course; the omelettes were divine, let me tell you, but that's not what you're here for. I opened the first notebook and started writing. Everything I was thinking and feeling, completely unfiltered. Nobody would ever read it, not even me. My intention was to throw the notebooks away before I left, but I needed to get everything out. All the anger at everything and everyone who could have stopped this happening, including myself. The pain of the loss and how this would affect the rest of my life. Everything I wanted to say to people who'd reacted in completely human ways when it had all happened, but their words still hurt. It all needed to come out. I wrote non-stop for hours before realising something else monumental had happened. I'd missed lunch. Those ice cream Mars Bars came in handy.

For the next five days, I wrote everything I was feeling until the well ran dry. I had no desire to read it back, and probably couldn't, anyway. My writing is illegible at the best of times, let alone in a heightened emotional state. Between bursts of writing, I watched the box set of *Friends*, all uncut episodes with commentary, and ate far too many ice cream Mars Bars. I would leave the room to eat at mealtimes, taking a quiet table in the restaurant's corner, and occasionally go to the shop to buy, you've guessed it, more ice cream Mars Bars. Those were my only interactions with other human beings for five days. The hotel had an indoor pool and a gym for all those healthy people who were in training, but I had no inclination to use any of it. I just wanted to escape into another world, which was comfortable, but with some added extras. Then I would have more bursts of writing and the cycle would repeat. Despite eating my weight in ice cream Mars Bars, I still lost almost a stone in weight that week. That's how sick I was.

On day six, I was craving prolonged sunlight on my skin, so I went for a walk along the promenade. My sleep had been erratic the past few days, so I was up early, which meant it was quiet, except for a few people running. Good for them! There is something about a sea breeze, the smell of the ocean and the feel of early morning sun on your skin that makes you content. It's not for everyone, and I am one of those 'It's too hot!' people when it passes a certain threshold, but for the first time since I'd been signed off sick, I was looking forward. I wasn't suddenly over my mother's death, and I never would be, but there had been a shift in my brain that enabled me to look forward optimistically. It wasn't just about how I would survive without her, but how I was going to live out the rest of my life in a way that wouldn't just make her proud, but so I could hold my own head high as well. It was time to return to the trenches and win back my man!

Rebirth Setback

The next six months were a challenge. Actually, that's underselling it; they were hell on earth! Okay, I'm being dramatic, but work life was a daily battle for me because my boss was the spawn of Lucifer. There was no other way to describe her. Life outside of work was moving forward with two big life events: moving house and getting married.

It is possible to keep work and home life separate, but it's not something you can do forever, especially if one of them is toxic. One is going to affect the other, and that's what happened.

Going back to work after my time out, I felt a sense of renewal. I wanted to move forward, but was hit by the first barrier. My performance rating was lowered because I'd not been in the office to deliver the rest of my objectives. 'My mother died six months ago, and I had a breakdown because of it, and you penalised me. Do you even have a heart?' is what I said in my head. What I actually said was, 'Okay,' and moved forward. Of course, I vented my frustrations to friends and family, but I was in a precarious situation. I wasn't financially set up to walk away, and I was recovering from a mental health setback; now was not the time to look for another job. Added to that, I needed stable employment to get a mortgage. There was no choice. I had to stay put. My boss held all the power, and I had to just shut up and keep delivering.

Over the next six months, things deteriorated further. Being patronised, gaslighted and undermined every day became torturous. For someone who struggles to regulate their emotions with medication, and an

ADHD diagnosis, imagine what I was like when I was undiagnosed, and unmedicated back then – a ticking time bomb!

There is an upside to being trapped in a job you can't leave, in that you have to find coping mechanisms. I had to stay and make the best of it. If I did something, it could backfire on me at the worst possible time, and blow up my entire life again! How did I mitigate the impact this person was having on me? It was a great lesson. I have passed on to hundreds of people I have coached over the years that if you can't change someone's behaviour, then change how you allow it to affect you. That is what you have control over. So, that's what I did.

Punchbags at the gym were an effective way of working out my frustrations, and there are added health benefits from exercise, or so I hear. Finding a safe space to bitch and moan with a kindred spirit develops lifelong friendships, and letting your imagination run wild in a fictional world is a great way to turn a hobby into a side hustle. These were all things I did over those six months, but when other people were affected by this person, and the wedding and house move were behind me, I knew it was time to put my head above the parapet and fight.

Superpower Discovery

Putting in a grievance against your boss is not a straightforward thing to do, but it had to be done. Why should I be the one to walk away? I had done nothing wrong, just existed. The fact that other people were being affected by this person's behaviour was a relief because it meant it wasn't personal, but that didn't make it right. I knew there could be consequences for doing this, but I'd hit the point where I knew walking away wasn't an option. I wouldn't be able to live with myself if I didn't do something. The downside of ADHD, for me at least, is we don't do things by halves. I didn't just make a complaint; I chose the nuclear option.

I won't get into the next few months but, yes, you read that right - months! These processes can be long, but the outcome was that I started a new year with a new boss. Her reason for leaving was apparently unrelated, and it may have been, I'll never know, but I like to think I'd done something positive by fighting back. But how did I get through that challenging year with a chaotic work environment and major life events going on outside of work: death, moving house, and marriage?

When I first thought about writing this book, I reflected on major life events which shifted my mindset and made me adopt new strategies for coping with challenges. There have been other traumatic events in my life, but I kept coming back to that year. After a catalogue of major events, both good and bad, happening in a short space of time, I was changed forever as a person. That's when I unconsciously developed my superpowers.

I'd always been able to **hyper-focus** on things which interested me, but now I could do it with anything I set my mind to. A good example was when I was criticised for arriving and leaving on time when my peers were working excessive hours. I was given more work as apparently it was clear I wasn't busy enough, so I made sure everything was still done inside my contracted hours. This led to more frustration from my boss, as she piled more and more work on me. And what did I do? I delivered it all without doing a minute of overtime. Yes, I felt very smug about it.

Being **organised** is something I have always found easier than others. However, I know I can become overbearing and control freak-y if I am stressed. The belief that nobody could do it better than me will creep in when I am under pressure. I'm a lot more self-aware now than I was back then, but it still happens. The only difference is that now I can recognise it and do something about it before it derails me too much.

In the situation with my boss piling the work on, I realised she would not shift her focus onto the others who were struggling with their workload. The fault was mine for being efficient, of course, so I went and supported my colleagues with some techniques which worked for me in being able to get stuff done. From a young age, my approach had always been that if I didn't understand something, I would learn it. I'd read many books on organisation and planning, and cherry-picked all the bits I liked best to come up with the Nick approach. Don't worry, it now has a catchier name, which we'll get onto later.

Sharing this model with my colleagues helped them to manage their workload better, and those techniques became my blueprint for creating the **time management** training courses I would design and deliver to hundreds of people throughout my career.

I can be scatterbrained, and that's putting it mildly. The sentence I say all the time which drives my husband mad is 'Have you seen my phone?' which I repeat several times a week. However, when you are building a case against someone, you need to develop techniques to ensure your **working memory** doesn't let you down. You can make notes, of course, but you'll still need to recall things you haven't thought about, especially when going through a grievance process. The trick was to focus on feelings. If I could associate actions with my emotional response to them, it would trigger the memory recall.

A conversation I've had with hundreds of managers over the years is when they complain that someone, or several people, in their team aren't **adapting to change**. My response is usually, 'So they are acting like a human being,' which is the reality. No matter what anyone says, as humans, our instinct is to resist change. We can develop resilience skills, and some can adapt quicker than others, but as a species, we like our comfort zone. Throw in ADHD and the concept of change has us running for the hills, especially if it is being imposed on us. Spend a year with a boss who was as unpredictable as the voting public has been over the last decade, and you have to learn to adapt quickly.

Finally, we come to **self-regulation,** which is definitely my biggest ADHD barrier. It's the one I struggle with the most, even to this day, but when you're in a situation where you have too much to lose if you allow everything to blow up, it becomes a huge motivator to get better at it, not that I recommend fear as a self-development tactic.

This isn't about suppressing your emotions, as that isn't healthy for anyone, but about finding a suitable outlet to express them. Am I a black belt in this superpower? Definitely not. This one is still very much a work in progress, but as I've climbed the career ladder and witnessed all the politics which are embedded in the DNA of the corporate world, the fact I can keep my mouth shut when I need to, and navigate all the drama to influence my desired outcome, is something I'm immensely proud of.

Action

If you don't have a journal, get one. Or if you have one, which is more like a diary, get another. Use it to write what you are thinking and feeling about anything and everything. The intention is to never read it back. You could even throw it away when you've finished, but it gives you an outlet to process all the chaos which is going on in your head. It's for your eyes only, so keep it somewhere safe, or be like me and have writing that is so illegible nobody will ever be able to read it.

What's next?

We're going to get into the science stuff. Don't you dare close this book. I'll make it interesting and quick – there's a joke in there! We'll cover the six executive functions of the brain so you can understand where the superpowers come from.

Chapter 3

The Science Stuff

This chapter covers the science bit. Not in lots of detail, because that would send me to sleep, but it's important to know the six executive functions of the brain aren't a theory from some rando, but are grounded in psychological research. How I've flipped these and turned them into superpowers is all on me. There are a variety of labels for the executive functions, so what I have used may not be ones you're familiar with, but the descriptions should be. I'm not a psychologist, and don't claim to be. I want to make this book as accessible to as many people as possible, and make a clear distinction between the ADHD superpowers. Yes, there is overlap, but each one stands alone, so you can choose which areas to focus on first, and not get overwhelmed by feeling you have to do everything at once.

Working as a learning and development professional for over twenty years, I've heard many a leader or individual contributor bang on about developing their weaknesses, and I don't disagree with that approach, but what about your strengths? The strengths you bring to the table are your unique selling point. That's why you got the job. You didn't get a job because of your weaknesses. You were hired despite them. People don't focus enough on their strengths. I was running a training session on time management with a group of graduates a few weeks ago, and this was a point I made to them. They have no, or limited, professional experience at this stage of their career and were hired for their potential and the strengths they showed in the assessment process. It's something they need to remember as they progress in their careers. Yes, develop your weaknesses, but keep enhancing your strengths as well.

I can't bang on enough about how this is the approach you should take as you learn about the superpowers. Don't just go straight to the one which is your weakness and disregard the others. I will never be that black belt in emotional regulation no matter how hard I try, but I dare anyone to try to out-organise me with Post-its and a whiteboard!

Executive Functions

Think of the brain as a command centre. It is working all the time, processing information at a million miles an hour. This helps us to plan, focus, adapt and regulate our behaviours. These functions guide our ability to complete tasks, solve problems, and interact with the world. Whether it's meeting that deadline, staying focused in a mind-numbing meeting, or adjusting to yet another process change because the powers that be didn't think it through the first time, executive functions shape success in both professional and personal life. While people with ADHD often experience additional challenges in these areas, they also possess strengths that, when harnessed, can become true superpowers.

Attention Control

This is about our ability to filter distractions, maintain focus, and shift attention when necessary. You know those people who can read a book in the middle of a crowd, or aren't constantly reaching for their phone to see if anyone liked that hilarious cat meme they posted earlier? I'll confess something: halfway through writing that sentence I checked my phone, and I haven't even posted a cat meme. And this is one of my strengths, people. Damn my ADHD brain and its love of shiny things. This phone is less than a week old and I have only dropped it three times so far. That is definite progress.

At work, attention control allows us to concentrate on the priorities while tuning out all the distractions of people gabbing in the surrounding office. This is not an easy feat. Why do you think people have their headphones on? This is why hybrid working leads to greater productivity; it's science! But let's not open that can of worms.

'In my day, I learnt from being in the office and listening to everything.'

'Well, your day was before the internet, so let's try another way.'

'It's the best way to learn. Look at what it did for me.'

'You know that *embracing change* thing you're always banging on about? Try practising what you preach.'

'Oh!'

This may or may not be an extract from a conversation I've had several times with senior leaders.

Many people struggle with sustaining focus, especially in environments overloaded with stimulation. Some people can work in a noisy office, and others work best in total silence. There is no perfect solution for everyone. We are all different. It's important to remember that great minds *don't* think alike.

Planning and Organisation

Setting goals, creating structures and establishing systems for efficiency are what this executive function is all about. This one is my time to shine. If everyone could do this, I wouldn't have needed to deliver hundreds of training sessions on this very topic. It is one many people struggle with to varying degrees. It's also the one where everyone has their own system and believes it is better than anybody else's.

Not to be mistaken with time management, which is up next, planning and organisation is getting things done, and knowing how to prioritise for maximum productivity. Do you know when you are the most productive? Do you jump out of bed in the morning full of energy? Or are you someone who wakes up after lunch but then doesn't switch off until the early hours? Whichever you are, you need to use your preferences to your advantage.

I couldn't cover this executive function without referencing the to-do list. Who doesn't love a list? I'm still not a fan of a digital version, as I love crossing things out with a pen, but I can make both work. I have lists about lists, and more so. There can never be too many lists in this world. Someone once told me they didn't believe in to-do lists, and I clutched my metaphorical pearls. They said they could just remember everything they needed to do. How is that possible?

Time Management

This is about how effectively we organise our hours, structure our tasks, and make sure we actually do the things we intend to do, rather than realising at midnight that we forgot something. You know that person who somehow always crams every single thing into their day without breaking a sweat? What do we think of those people? I love them, as long as they aren't gloating and making me look bad.

This is one of my neutral areas. I know how to manage time well. I have trained people on time management, developed models for it and can talk about it for hours. But there are times when a deadline doesn't exist until I am reminded of it and run around the house shouting expletives. That's ADHD for you. One moment you are convinced you have all the time in the world, the next you are wondering how you have done absolutely nothing all day other than watch random YouTube videos on how well Madonna's backlist has performed over the decades. I will neither confirm nor deny whether that has actually happened!

Time management is not just about knowing what to do, it's about implementing systems that work for your brain. Some people thrive with detailed planners, some need external deadlines and others use sheer panic as their greatest motivator. If you struggle with time blindness, a truly infuriating thing which is very real, this is a superpower you should prioritise as it can work like a ripple effect on the others.

Working Memory

Working memory is the unsung hero of executive functions. It is your brain's ability to hold onto and recall information in real time. It's basically remembering what you're supposed to be doing while you're doing it. People with strong working memory can juggle multiple thoughts, hold onto details from meetings without writing everything down. I hate those people! I'm joking, of course, but why can I recall an insignificant detail from a conversation in 1997, but not remember what I said I would email my boss five minutes ago?

Picture this: you walk into a room to do something very important. You have total confidence in what you were about to do. Then it's gone. Vanished into the void. You stand there staring at nothing, knowing only that something was supposed to happen, but it has left your brain never to be seen again. You eventually leave, and five minutes later, the memory returns. I retrace my steps, looking for the memory trigger, and this is where the aforementioned 'Where's my phone?' comes from.

Working memory struggles mean losing track of conversations, forgetting instructions and having to revisit the same information multiple times. Some people compensate with notes, reminders and excessive Post-its, while others rely on external memory systems. I salute the people with fifteen different productivity apps. I probably have the same, but have forgotten what I have downloaded. At last check, I had over two hundred apps on my phone, and probably use less than twenty regularly - oops.

Cognitive Flexibility

This is the ability to adapt, shift perspectives, and problem-solve in the moment. Some people love change, others fight it as though their life depends on it, but here's the truth: flexibility is an undeniable strength.

I like to think I'm adaptable, but I also instinctively resist when my plans are thrown into chaos. When someone shifts a deadline suddenly, I must mentally reset myself. Translation: I need a moment to scream silently at the inconvenience before embracing the new plan. And that's just me being honest, because we all have moments where rigidity feels safer than change. I'm a big fan of change when I am the one driving it, but come to me with a last-minute pivot which makes no sense, and I am imagining you as victim number three in my next crime novel.

Cognitive flexibility means learning how to adapt gracefully rather than begrudgingly, adjusting strategies on the go and remaining calm when things inevitably change. Without it, life feels like a series of disappointments, missed opportunities and frustrating roadblocks. Resilience is a critical skill for everyone. Change is a constant thing at work and outside it. There is no choice now but to jump on the change train. Next stop, my sanity.

Impulse Control

I've saved the worst for last. Yes, you read that right. This is my nemesis. My weakest executive function. My undoing many times. It's a daily occurrence and most of the time it's manageable, but when I break, it's this executive function which is driving the bus off the cliff.

Some people naturally regulate their impulses. They think before they speak, consider consequences before acting, and rarely make reckless decisions. How do they do that? Then there are the rest of us. Who occasionally, or should that be frequently, buy something completely unnecessary, say the first thing that pops into our head or realise halfway through eating an entire pizza that maybe we should have stopped at two slices. To be fair, that's a lie. Who would ever stop at two slices of pizza?

Impulse control is especially challenging for ADHD brains, because dopamine-driven decision-making is a real thing. We love the instant reward, the quick gratification and that future consequences can wait until later. It's like a drug and we're big addicts for dopamine. It's why I set limits for anything which can be overindulged. This could be drinks or a night in a casino on a cruise ship - again, oops!

I know my weaknesses, and impulsivity is big. My husband is no better. Whenever we book a holiday, we have to factor in an additional budget, as we're likely to be hit with amendment fees when we change our minds, which happens more often than not.

Fortunately, I am living proof that impulse control can be trained, and there are ways to slow down the decision-making process, ensuring rational choices win out over emotional reactions. Will I still occasionally say the brutally honest thing I probably should have phrased differently? Of course. I mean, wouldn't life be boring if we were all logical all the time?

Blueprint Cocktail

I hope that wasn't too detailed. I kept the technical jargon out of it as much as I could, but wanted to bring the executive functions to life for you. This will help you understand the six superpowers and what their intention is.

With the brain, it has often been referred to as a blueprint for how we function as a human. I like to think of it more like a cocktail. Now, how do I explain this analogy and maintain my credibility? Have you seen those social media posts where people are filling up different cups with parts of their personality, or even regarding their sexuality? The joke is that they overfill or under fill one cup as a visual gag about who they are. I think of my ADHD brain and executive functions in the same way.

If I take myself as an example: attention control and planning and organisation, that cup would have spillage for me. The bartender has overfilled and you're having to slurp the overspill. Then you have working memory and impulse control and I'm shouting, 'Where is my drink?' because the glass is dry. There is no individual who has all those cups perfectly balanced.

Do you know someone who can do all this?

1. Sit through a three-hour meeting without checking their phone once and skim a 50-page report, pulling out the key details in less time than you take to get your third coffee of the morning.
2. Plan their calendar six months in advance, have a colour-coded to-do list and arrive at meetings early, even though their diary is back-to-back.
3. Start a task, knowing exactly how long it will take them. There is no procrastination or time blindness, just precise execution of getting the job done.
4. Know every client's name, every project deadline and that one time someone promised to bring in their homemade cookies, but never did. It was three years ago.
5. Have no problem with their boss changing the entire project five minutes before the deadline. They seamlessly pivot, problem-solve and still deliver on time with options better than the original.

6. Never send passive-aggressive emails, don't eat six cupcakes from the staffroom just because they are there and maintain complete composure when someone asks for 'one more change' on a project that has just been signed off after months of pain and suffering.

This person does not exist and, if they do, I want to meet them and understand their DNA lineage and when cloning will be ethical.

The ADHD brain will be skewed in that we find some of these executive functions incredibly challenging, no matter how hard we try, and sometimes we just can't do something. This is debilitating for some, and others can do enough to get by. Then, we have other executive functions which are turbo-charged. These can be viewed as a priceless strength by some and seen as a negative by others, depending on how we use them. Perfection doesn't exist, and we need to focus on what is right for us, rather than trying to make everyone happy, because nobody has the superpower to achieve that.

Action

One of the best ways to understand your executive functions is to take an online test to assess where your strengths lie and which areas need improvement. There is no one test I would recommend as there are new ones all the time. A good executive function assessment should ask at least fifty questions. Do your research and look at reviews, rather than be tempted by that shiny advert on social media. We've all been there!

What's next?

We're going to look at the six superpowers and summarise what they are. Each one will have its own dedicated chapter later on, where I will share my cheat codes. But, for now, let's give you a quick overview of what the meat of this book is all about.

Chapter 4

The Six Superpowers

In this chapter, I'll summarise what each superpower is, and which executive function it's supercharging. Later in the book, we'll go into more depth on each superpower, as well as the cheat codes I have created, because as ADHDers, we do love a short cut!

The six superpowers are:

1. **Focus Beam** - the ability to lock on a target, regardless of how interesting it is, and not stop until you've reached your goal.

2. **Vision Crafter** - the ability to create precise plans, without procrastinating, which guarantee success.

3. **Time Warp** - the ability to control time, rather than let it control you, so you can get everything done.

4. **Mind Vault** - the ability to recall knowledge and information at the time you need it most, and not have it lost in the ether forever.

5. **Mental Morph** - the ability to adapt to any situation without breaking out in a cold sweat, and running for the hills.

6. **Impulse Shield** - the ability to deflect your impulses, no matter how much you are pushed, and show up as a calm, logical and rational adult.

I'm sure you have heard of the saying 'Jack of all trades, master of none'. So, that's not what we're going for here. You should only focus on two superpowers at once. One should be the executive function which is holding you back. This might not be your weakest, but one which has the biggest impact on your life, whether that is personal or work. The other should be something you're already strong at. This is what makes you brilliant, so don't neglect it by focusing elsewhere. Things change and develop rapidly in today's world, so don't neglect the existing strengths which already make you stand out. It would be like The Flash decided not to do any running training. Thankfully, running is not my superpower. I get far too distracted and have almost died several times on a treadmill when something or someone caught my attention. Now, before I veer off into a random tangent about running, let's get into each of these superpowers.

Focus Beam

At work, we have endless notifications pinging at us, conversations overlap, and the lure of social media is just a thumb movement away. Mastering this superpower can be the difference between peak productivity and an afternoon spent searching for the perfect allotment, even though you once had a cactus which died – true story!

Having the power of Focus Beam means you can lock onto tasks like a laser beam (see what I did there!), and absorb important details without being derailed by irrelevant crap, or stimuli, if you're being polite. This superpower allows you to tune out distractions, whether it's an office conversation about someone's neighbour's dog who keeps pooping on their lawn, or that little envelope which means an unread email is trying to lure you like a siren song, saying it could be from the CEO. Newsflash: the CEO doesn't email you. And if you're not an executive, you should be nervous if they do.

What happens when you don't develop this superpower? Imagine trying to finish an important report while your mind jumps between checking the latest cat memes, remembering you forgot to send a birthday message out of a sense of duty to that friend you haven't seen for a decade, or wondering whether someone will ever invent a stapler that doesn't jam and force you to bang it on the table accompanied by a harmony of expletives. Just me? Didn't think so!

Without Focus Beam, you become the human embodiment of a browser with forty-seven open tabs, none of which are productive but all of which are draining your energy. Tasks take twice as long, deadlines sneak up like that annoying friend who always scares you and workplace efficiency tanks. In meetings, your brain drifts off mid-discussion, and the dreaded 'Wait, what are we talking about again?' moment strikes. Ultimately, your ability to absorb critical information, process details effectively, and execute tasks efficiently suffers, leading to increased stress and last-minute panic sessions.

For we ADHDers, Focus Beam is both a gift and a challenge. ADHD brains struggle with regulating attention, meaning distraction can be overwhelming. The smallest environmental trigger, such as the tap of a keyboard, the movement of a colleague or the sight of a bird outside, can derail thoughts completely. Although birds can be very interesting when compared to responding to an audit action. On the flip side, hyper-focus can kick in, turning attention into an unstoppable force, but only when the brain decides the task is interesting enough. Definitely not said audit action.

Someone with ADHD can spend five hours meticulously organising their music playlist while struggling to complete an urgent report that is due because it's about something regulatory. I mean, seriously, who finds that stuff interesting? But with the power of Focus Beam, you can get the stuff done that usually makes you want to stab your eyeballs with a knitting needle. Apologies for the visual, but am I lying?

Vision Crafter

Vision Crafter is the superpower of planning and organisation. It's being able to turn ideas into structured, achievable goals, instead of those same goals we have again and again. How many of you have made the same new year's resolutions for over a decade? I'll just hide in the corner!

Whether it is crafting a long-term strategy or simply ensuring day-to-day tasks are completed efficiently, this superpower is all about making things happen with precision and intent. While some people instinctively structure their thoughts and priorities with ease, others drown in half-started projects, forgotten deadlines and chaotic to-do lists. Anyone else got a shed full of different coloured paints because your husband had a 'great idea' and then lost interest?

The power of Vision Crafter means that life feels less overwhelming. Work becomes more manageable, and there is a clear sense of progress rather than a perpetual feeling of scrambling to keep up. When this superpower is developed, deadlines no longer feel like surprise attacks, goals are carefully mapped out and there is a sense of clarity when deciding.

Without this superpower, life feels like an unscripted improvisation; sometimes exhilarating, but mostly exhausting. Tasks pile up, responsibilities become entangled and everything is handled on a last-minute basis. Deadlines sneak up unnoticed, projects never quite get finished and the weight of constant disorganisation becomes mentally draining. Those without planning skills often find themselves overwhelmed by their own workload, unable to prioritise effectively or expect what is coming next.

Many people with ADHD struggle with task initiation, finding it hard to start projects even when they know they need to. The overwhelming number of steps involved in planning can lead to avoidance, with the brain simply choosing not to deal with it until urgency forces action, which could be a Teams message from your boss asking, 'Where is that report?' and you run around screaming, before attempting to produce something out of thin air in a nanosecond. I definitely didn't do that last week!

Time Warp

Time Warp is the superpower of time management; the ability to perceive, allocate, and optimise time to tasks. Time management and prioritisation are often bundled together, but they are unique skills. For some, managing time feels effortless. They instinctively know how to structure their day, pace their workload and avoid the dreaded last-minute panic.

Having the Time Warp superpower means work becomes predictable rather than chaotic. Deadlines are met with calm efficiency and there is a sense of having control over tasks instead of them controlling you. Those with strong time management skills don't feel constantly overwhelmed because they structure their workload in a way that prevents bottlenecks and last-minute stress.

Bosses, colleagues, and clients appreciate those who can balance priorities and maintain efficiency, making this superpower one of the most sought-after workplace strengths. It is also one everyone wants to work on. I've never run a time management training session in the past twenty years which wasn't at capacity, with a waiting list.

ADHD makes Time Warp one of the most difficult superpowers to control because time perception is inconsistent. A task that should take five minutes might somehow stretch into an hour, while an entire afternoon disappears in what feels like ten minutes. Many people with ADHD struggle with estimating time accurately, leading to either wild optimism such as, 'This will only take ten minutes,' or complete avoidance. 'Just another five minutes on TikTok. Why is it dark outside?'

Time Warp is one of the most empowering superpowers to develop. Those who are strong at time management become highly effective professionals, trusted to deliver results on schedule and with confidence. Strong time management builds resilience, focus and productivity. Fortunately, time management is a skill that can be learned, even for those who struggle with this executive function.

Mind Vault

Mind Vault is the superpower of working memory; the ability to hold and recall information in real time, and keep track of multiple pieces of information simultaneously. This can include random things which have no purpose. For example, I have no idea why I can still remember the postcode from the house I stopped living at when I was seven years old.

Some people seem to have an effortless ability to store and retrieve details, juggling multiple tasks while remembering everything from important deadlines to what their colleague said in passing two weeks ago. Others rely on frantic note-taking and sheer luck to avoid forgetting what they were supposed to be doing. Before hot desking became common, there was always that person whose desk looked like a stationery shop had vomited on it.

Without Mind Vault, life becomes a game of trying to hold onto information that keeps slipping away. Forgetting details, losing track of tasks and struggling to recall important conversations makes work and daily life frustrating. This leads to inefficient task execution, requiring frequent reconfirmation of details or retracing previous steps. In meetings, forgetting key points leads to repeated clarification requests, while deadlines and commitments feel scattered rather than structured. This does not make you popular with your colleagues. If one more person puts a meeting in my diary to share a spreadsheet on screen to talk through line by line, I may never stop screaming.

ADHD brains often compensate by creating external memory systems, such as extensive note-taking, reminders and physical cues to trigger recall. I like visual prompts to remind me to do something, but that often clashes with a husband who likes to tidy those visual triggers away.

When this superpower is mastered, work feels less overwhelming, decision-making becomes faster, and recall becomes a powerful skill rather than a constant frustration. The Mind Vault superpower also comes in handy when a decision maker forgets something they already agreed to. Being able to play back how a conversation went will often trigger their recall, and you can feel very smug about it.

Mental Morph

Mental Morph is the superpower of cognitive flexibility. That sounds far too technical for me, but there was no other way to word that sentence. In short, this is the ability to adapt to new information, shift perspectives and embrace change with ease. Which ADHDer embraces change willingly? Yeah, didn't think so.

Some people seem to thrive in unpredictable situations, adjusting effortlessly when plans change or when new ideas challenge their assumptions. I admire these people greatly, and also envy them intensely. I'm a big lover of change, if I'm the one driving it, of course.

Others, meaning me, can struggle with rigid thought patterns, resisting change and feeling overwhelmed when unexpected obstacles arise. Mental Morph is the superpower that separates those who can confidently pivot and adapt from those who find themselves frozen by shifting circumstances, or who will use distractions as classic avoidance.

Having the Mental Morph superpower means that change is not something to fear, but an opportunity for innovation and growth. People with this superpower can approach challenges from multiple angles, shifting strategies when needed rather than forcing an approach that no longer works.

Without Mental Morph, life feels frustratingly rigid. Change becomes overwhelming rather than manageable, leading to stress and difficulty navigating new situations. You may resist new technology, struggle with feedback or have difficulty shifting focus when circumstances require it.

ADHD brains can struggle with shifting gears quickly, leading to frustration when faced with unexpected changes. Task-switching may feel difficult, as the brain tends to hyper-focus on one thing at a time, making transitions mentally exhausting. Individuals with ADHD can also be incredibly adaptive in the right circumstances. When interested in the change, they can shift perspectives with ease, but if it's not engaging, then forget it. You lost us the moment you shared a spreadsheet with seven thousand columns on your screen.

Impulse Shield

Impulse Shield is the superpower of self-regulation – the ability to manage impulses, emotions, and behaviours in a way that leads to thoughtful decision-making rather than reactive responses. Wouldn't that be nice?

This superpower supports the executive function that allows someone to pause before acting, assess the situation with clarity and choose a measured response rather than making a rash decision they might later regret. Some people seem to have an instinctive ability to regulate their emotions, resist distractions and remain composed even in high-pressure situations. Others, also me, blurt out the first thing that comes to mind, clicking 'Add to basket' on yet another unnecessary purchase, or struggling to hold back frustration when faced with an irritating colleague. Remind me again how I work in HR?

This superpower is invaluable in the workplace. It leads to better communication, stronger leadership, and more effective teamwork. Being able to regulate emotions means conflicts are handled constructively rather than escalating unnecessarily. People with strong impulse control build reputations for being reliable, level-headed, and able to navigate challenging situations with confidence.

Those who struggle with self-regulation often make impulsive decisions, whether it is speaking before thinking, spending money they should have saved or abandoning a long-term goal in favour of an immediate distraction.

ADHD brains process emotions quickly, making it harder to filter immediate reactions before acting on them. There is often a powerful urge to say what comes to mind instantly, click on distractions without thinking, or react emotionally before fully assessing the situation. Impulse-driven behaviour can frustrate, especially when the consequences are undesirable.

This spontaneity can also be a strength. ADHD individuals are often creative and quick-thinking. The challenge is learning when to embrace impulsivity and when to rein it in to prevent unnecessary setbacks. Being completely open, this superpower is my nemesis and probably always will be. However, the one thing which helps the most is that I accepted it a long time ago, and do everything I can to not let it blow things up too often.

Unlimited Power

There's always one character in a superhero story who thinks they can take on everything, wielding all the power without consequence, only to realise, often too late, that no one can handle it all at once. Whether it's a villain grasping for ultimate control or a hero trying to carry the weight of the world, the message is simple: trying to control everything at once is a recipe for disaster.

Executive functions are complex, and while developing them is powerful, it is unrealistic to expect instant mastery in every single one. No one, not even the most hyper-organised, super-efficient, emotionally stable professional, has every executive function working perfectly all the time. Instead of forcing yourself into an unattainable ideal of flawless productivity, focus on recognising what already makes you extraordinary and refine the area that is holding you back from achieving your goals.

Action

List all six superpowers in order, starting with the one you think is your strongest and working down to your weakest. Once you've completed this, leave it to one side for a week or whenever you have read the detailed chapters on each of the superpowers, whichever is longer. Look at the list again, and make any revisions and produce your definitive list, which will help inform you where you need to focus first.

What's next?

Before we get into each superpower, I'm going to share a little secret with you. Think of it as the cherry on top of an already delicious cake. What is the secret sauce for mastering your ADHD superpowers?

Chapter 5

The Secret Sauce

You hear the term 'secret sauce' often when companies talk about their brand or USP. What is it that makes them special? This isn't about the seven million spices that make you want to lick your fingers, but more about that extra ingredient which enhances everything. For some people, it's ketchup. I remember someone adding it to a roast dinner once, and thought it unusual, but who am I to judge? Then they added it to mac and cheese, and I was judge, jury and executioner – WTAF!

But we're not here to talk about ketchup. The secret sauce to enhancing your superpowers is the skill of **emotional intelligence**. Now, before you go, 'But I don't have it,' that's complete bollocks. Can I swear in a non-fiction book? It's my book, so I can do what I want. Let's bust a few myths immediately.

1. Emotional intelligence is not something you have or you don't have – we all have it. It's just some of us are better at using it than others.
2. It is a skill, and therefore it can be developed. It is not something you are born with, and that's it. A bit like the whole 'Leaders are born, not made' mantra that was doing the rounds a few decades ago. We all know what we think of that now, don't we?
3. Emotional intelligence has many facets. Just because someone has high empathy skills does not mean all the facets of their emotional intelligence are high. Some people can be incredibly empathetic and caring, but inside they're a hot mess.
4. Nobody is born a fully rounded human being. Our influences and experiences shape us. These elements help form our core personality and will affect how challenging it will be for us to develop our emotional intelligence.
5. You can still develop your superpowers even without strong emotional intelligence. It's a secret sauce that will enhance your powers further, but it isn't something you must have in order to succeed.

EQ versus IQ

There was a time when your IQ score was the primary indicator of success. Intelligence, logic and problem-solving ability were what would propel you to be the next CEO. Having these core skills meant you could deal with any challenge, and still be strong and respected as a leader. Do we still think that?

One thing I am not doing here is pooh-poohing IQ. Those skills are still very important, and will help you be successful in your career, but they won't do it alone. IQ measures cognitive abilities, such as how well you process information, how quickly you grasp concepts, how strong your reasoning skills are and so on. However, it does not translate into effective decision-making, self-regulation or social awareness. You can be a brilliant intellectual, but struggle to manage your emotions and communicate poorly.

Emotional intelligence, also referred to as EQ, is your ability to understand, regulate and use emotions effectively, not just in yourself, but in others. There are many explanations of what emotional intelligence is, but I've found the one which people have grasped the easiest in the training room is that there are three parts to emotional intelligence:

1. **Self-awareness:** You've got butterflies in your stomach, your palms are sweaty or your heart is pounding. Why? Knowing why we are

feeling different emotions is crucial to developing our self-awareness.

2. **Awareness of others:** Ever heard the term 'Read the room'? Or have you ever been in a meeting and been told 'Yes' but it doesn't feel right? That's your intuition picking up on other people's emotions. Being able to pick up on what is being said, how it is being said, and what is not being said is a crucial skill in any workplace.

3. **Managing and adapting your emotions**: This is where the 'intelligence' part comes in. Knowing when to be quiet, when to walk away, when your problem isn't important or switching from angry to empathetic is what we're talking about here. This is the most challenging part, and something nobody gets right every time. You keep having to work at it.

The EQ-I 2.0 Model

I will not get into lots of detail here, but there are many EQ models out there and this is my favourite. I was accredited to do assessments and coach people on their results using this model in 2014, and have supported hundreds of people since then. The model breaks down EQ into five composites. Stay with me, people.

1. **Self-perception:** The inner self, and how we feel about ourselves. This is about being self-confident, understanding your emotions when you feel them and setting yourself goals to keep continuously improving.

2. **Self-expression:** The outer self and how we present ourselves to the world. This is about how you express your views and emotions in different situations.

3. **Interpersonal:** How we build relationships with others, show empathy and think about the bigger picture and wider impact of our actions. In a work setting, this is about considering the impact of decisions outside your siloed team bubble, but also being mindful of the impact of any decisions on the wider sector and community you work in.

4. **Decision-making:** How we use emotions in our decision-making. It's not about making emotional decisions, but about getting the balance right with logic and intuition. This includes how we approach problems, how we utilise our objectivity and how we manage our gut-feel reactions. It's a tricky balance getting those right, as our personality often dictates which we lean more towards.

5. **Stress management:** What it says on the tin. It incorporates flexibility, stress tolerance and optimism. Are we someone who can adapt to change easily? Do we have a high threshold for stress? Are we more of a glass half full or empty person? These are all things which can affect our stress levels.

That's enough on the model. It's a good one, so worth checking out if you want to learn more about yourself.

How EQ strengthens your ADHD superpowers

This is how a developed EQ can support each of the superpowers, so keep this in mind as you work through the rest of the book:

1. **Focus Beam:** You will be more easily able to identify when emotions are hijacking your attention, allowing you to prioritise focus time.
2. **Vision Crafter:** EQ strengthens self-motivation and discipline, which means you can plan and prioritise with a logical head and not be driven by impulses in response to emotions.
3. **Time Warp:** Being more in control of your emotions means you can allocate time to tasks in a considered way, and be assertive in pushing back when needed.
4. **Mind Vault:** Managing stress effectively means improved memory recall because your

brain isn't overloaded with emotional distractions.

5. **Mental Morph:** Developed EQ can make it less challenging to adapt to change, rather than resisting unfamiliar and uncomfortable situations out of fear.
6. **Impulse Shield:** Your EQ can help you pause before reacting, recognise your emotional triggers more easily and regulate impulsive urges before they become the main character.

Action

Complete an EQ assessment of some kind. There are lots of freebies out there. You would need a trained professional to do the EQ-I 2.0. The reports themselves aren't expensive, but the time for a coach to go through your results could be. Look for something which covers the three core areas of EQ: self-awareness, awareness of others and managing and adapting your emotions.

What's next?

The next part of the book will explore all the superpowers. What are the benefits of developing them, and drawbacks if you don't? How does each superpower impact people with ADHD? What personal effectiveness skills can you build to give you the foundations for each superpower? Last, but not least, you'll learn my cheat code for each ADHD superpower.

Chapter 6

The Power of Focus Beam

Focus Beam is the ability to cut through distractions, stay locked into a task, and shift attention with precision when needed. It's tied directly to attention control, one of the most essential executive functions for productivity, learning and performance.

But let's be honest, staying focused is hard. There is always something trying to pull attention away: notifications, emails, conversations, food, or is that just me?

This is not just about forcing yourself to concentrate, you need to create an environment where focus is easier. This includes minimising distractions before they take over, and knowing when to shift approach rather than endless flip flopping between things because we get bored, or something new and shiny plays into our magpie tendencies.

From speaking to other ADHDers, they regard their ability to hyper-focus as their ultimate superpower. This is the executive function I hear the term 'superpower' used about the most, but are they using it to its full potential? I have always had moments when I can hyper-focus. One I refer to most is when I wrote the first draft of an eighty-thousand-word novel in ten days. But that was easy, because I was interested in it. How do you activate the power when the task is super deluxe mega boring? We could probably all name at least ten work tasks immediately which would go on that list.

The benefits of Focus Beam

This might seem obvious, but developing strong attention control can completely transform your efficiency at work. The benefits are endless, but let's focus on five, namely because I like things in multiples of five, which I recently discovered is driven by my autism. Perhaps one to unpack in the next book.

1. **Increased productivity:** With the power of Focus Beam, we can sustain our attention span on important tasks, and fight off distractions, such as that ping from the dating app notification – I won't tell anybody. The point is, focusing on more meaningful tasks, rather than what I refer to as 'pointless busy work', leads to better outcomes, which affects productivity. I know dating is not

pointless busy work, but I remember it feeling like that sometimes. At least those days are behind me. From what I've heard from friends it sounds even more exhausting these days, so I feel for you.

2. **Better decision-making:** Focus Beam enables you to apply a filter to background noise, so it doesn't distract you. Some people need total silence to focus, and others need something humming along. I'm writing this with the radio on in the background and even though they are playing a proper bop from Madonna right now, my Focus Beam is turned on. That sounded better in my head! But, by staying focused on the task in hand, which is what I am trying to do here, we are less tempted to make a reckless decision as our brain is engaged in task execution and not being driven by emotions.
3. **Improved learning and retention:** As a learning and development professional, I know the importance of this one. To aid retention, particularly in adults, you need to keep interest in the subject, but it also needs to feel like a worthwhile use of time. Yes, make training fun, but remember that fun is a subjective word. If you have to attend some important training and it's delivered by a subject expert, rather than a professional trainer, you are likely getting death by PowerPoint - we've all been there. By

harnessing your Focus Beam power, you will better concentrate on the content, extract the parts which are important to you, and retain them.

4. **Reduced stress:** Switching tasks all the time is mentally exhausting. Whoever coined the phrase 'multitasking' should be in prison – I joke, well ... kind of. First, the concept of multitasking implies you can do lots of things in parallel, but are any of them meaningful? Can you write a report, analyse data and do someone's appraisal meeting at the same time? Of course you can't. But if your brain is thinking about all of them at once, then your stress levels will increase and nothing will get the focused attention it deserves.
5. **Higher quality work:** Being able to churn through tasks quickly is great to get that to-do list down, but what does the quality look like? I've reviewed work from others which had silly mistakes. I try not to let it irritate me. It depends on my mood that day, but if it's repeated then it sets off a red flag for me that this person might be overworked and I need to offer support. You should take this approach with your own work. If you keep making obvious mistakes, something needs to give.

The drawbacks of not developing Focus Beam

Of course, we have to look at the flip side. This isn't about weaknesses, but more about the impact of not developing our Focus Beam superpower. Without strong attention control, work can feel like a never-ending battle against interruptions. Let's focus on five examples again, because, well, you know why.

1. **Chronic distraction:** It's easy for our focus to drift. I do it when people are speaking directly to me, which infuriates my husband and others. I can't help it sometimes, but if I am trying to get work done, it can lead to constant procrastination in that I am consciously looking for something to distract me. Without having the power of Focus Beam, this would be a never-ending loop.
2. **Mental fatigue:** Constant switching between tasks drains energy and depletes dopamine quickly. This means nothing gets completed properly as we are constantly looking for something more interesting to get our energy levels back up.
3. **Missed deadlines:** As well as being late, we can leave things half finished, especially when there are no consequences. At work, we have a manager with expectations of us. Outside work, the inability to focus means things are late, or they never get completed. There are probably millions of unfinished books out

there, which nobody else will ever get to read. Are you one of those people who always wanted to write a book?

4. **Overwhelm and anxiety:** Feeling scattered, struggling to concentrate, and being pulled in too many directions can make us feel overwhelmed and cause our anxiety to spike. ADHDers feel anxious often, it's like a default setting. Having the inability to focus on task execution can lead to us catastrophising the consequences, which are often exaggerated, but regardless will cause us to become overwhelmed.
5. **Reduced efficiency:** The inability to concentrate on task execution makes everything take longer than it should. What might take you an hour when you are utilising Focus Beam could take a week or longer as you give in to constant distractions, procrastinate and doom spiral.

Focus Beam isn't about forcing discipline, it's about designing a smarter way to control attention before it controls you.

ADHD and Focus Beam

As I mentioned earlier, for ADHDers this is often the executive function they refer to as their superpower, because we can hyper-focus for long, intense periods of time. Three people once replaced me when I left a job, after they'd refused my request for extra resources. Yes, I felt smug about it.

Staying focused is hard, especially when it's for something which is a snooze fest, or you are easily distracted. Does anyone else take three hours to watch a two-hour film? An actor appears on screen, and you remember them from something but can't think what it is. You look them up on IMDb, and remember they won an Oscar for something, so you quickly check Wikipedia, and see that they are related to an actress you really like. What was that film she was in? Ah, yes, back to IMDb. Oh, yes, I love that film. Do I have it on any of my streaming platforms? Oh no, it's on the one I don't have. Oh look, they are doing a thirty-day trial. I could get it, and watch the film, then cancel. Too much has then happened in the film that you need to rewind it, and you can feel your husband's eyes boring into you, with him wishing he had heat vision, like Superman. Ooh, how many people have played Superman? Back to Wikipedia. Is this anyone else, or just me?

So what is the cheat code for you to develop the superpower of Focus Beam? It's simple, all you need is some DOPE.

The DOPE Engine for hyper-focus

Of course, this is all with tongue firmly in cheek, but when I was developing this model and it came out as an acronym for DOPE, I knew it was a sign, and why? Because I'm a forty-something grown man who gives up control of my brain to my inner child more often than I should. So, are you ready to learn all about DOPE? Okay, I'll stop now.

DOPE stands for: distractions, organised, preference and endgame. It's referred to as an engine, rather just 'model' which is boring, but also because you need all four components of DOPE to get your Focus Beam motor running.

D = Distractions: eliminate the saboteurs

Hyper-focus can't happen if your brain is fighting off every distraction. That means:

1. Phone on silent, or thrown across the room, whatever works for you.
2. Close unnecessary tabs. If you have forty-seven browser windows open, you are setting yourself up for failure.
3. Block pop-ups, because one notification will ruin everything. The 'Do not disturb' on Teams is a wondrous invention.

This is your mental battlefield. If something competes for your attention, it's gotta go. That includes husbands and cats – sshhh, don't tell anyone I said that.

O = Organised: set the scene for productivity

Your brain can't hyper-focus if your workspace looks like a crime scene. Get everything ready before you start, so you don't spend thirty minutes searching for that one crucial document.

1. Clean desk, clear mind. Yes, it actually works.
2. Have your tools ready: laptop, notes, coffee, emotional stability.
3. Prep ahead. If you need research, have it to hand before the hyper-focus session starts.

When your environment is structured, your brain stops wasting energy on logistical chaos and just gets to work.

P = Preference: set the ambience that works for you

Some people need total silence. Others need their favourite playlist blasting in the background, because Beethoven and heavy metal both have their place in productivity. Heart 90s radio station is my jam.

Find what optimises your brain's engagement:

1. Music or no music?
2. Dim lighting or bright?
3. Background noise or headphones on?
4. Standing desk, sitting desk, or lying on the floor questioning existence?

Hyper-focus thrives when your brain is comfortable and stimulated just the right amount. Not overwhelmed and not bored stiff. Right now, I am sitting on my sofa in my home office, because the desk reminds me of the day job, and the radio is playing. There is a breeze coming in through the window and it's quiet outside. Perfect set-up for me.

E = Endgame: reward the victory

Hyper-focus isn't sustainable if you burn out without a pay-off. Motivation needs incentives. Before you start, set an endgame. Something fun, rewarding and guilt-free once you've completed your task:

1. Fifteen minutes of doom scrolling, because you deserve it.
2. Cake - self-explanatory.
3. A walk, a workout or just staring out of the window contemplating life.

If your brain knows there's something good at the end, it'll work harder to get there faster. For me, I am going to the coffee shop once I have finished this chapter to have a cupcake, coffee and to read my latest book, which I deliberately stopped reading at a juicy part. I know how my brain likes to be rewarded.

Why DOPE works

By removing distractions, structuring your space, setting the right ambience and rewarding progress, hyper-focus stops being accidental and starts becoming a controlled tool. It's easy to hyper-focus on something you are interested in, such as me writing this book. When I return to the day job next week, I have to review an eLearning course on risk management, which is about as exciting as having a root canal, but it needs to be done. I have blocked my diary out to get it done in the afternoon, made sure I will be in the right space and my reward will be that I can leave the office on time. It's not much, but getting home at six o'clock in the summer is a nice reward, and enough to motivate me to get it done.

The DOPE Engine ensures that focus isn't just luck. It's engineered for success and it's completely flexible in what works for you. You might be someone who works in total silence and their reward will be a kale smoothie, and I am not judging you, I promise. You do you, and I'll be wrapping up this chapter shortly and going for my cupcake. They better have some lemon flavour left or it will feel like the world has ended!

Not ready for DOPE?

It's important to recognise that not everyone can use DOPE immediately. Some people will struggle more with distractions, workspace organisation or even setting the right ambience. People look at me like I'm from another planet when they see how quickly I can churn work out, but I didn't come out of the womb with the power of Focus Beam. There's another sentence which sounded better in my head, but I'm leaving it in.

How do we build the foundations for developing Focus Beam and becoming a master of hyper-focus? You need to build up some of your core skills and think of these as foundations. Personal effectiveness skills are important because they can be utilised and deployed for different things. Your core skills are what will help you develop your superpowers.

There are a multitude of skills we could list out here, but we ADHDers don't have time for long lists. We're just going to focus on three core skills: self-awareness, task management and discipline. Yes, I didn't go for five here. I have a liking towards the number three as well, but not multiples of three. The idea of a list of nine things would bring me out in hives, but that's one to unpack later.

Self-awareness

You can't fix what you don't notice. Self-awareness means recognising when focus is slipping, understanding what triggers distractions and identifying how your brain works best. Knowing your biggest distraction triggers helps you develop strategies for eliminating them effectively. You may think you know what your distractions are, but you may be missing some. Recognise when your brain zones out, which for me is when my husband talks about his plans for the garden – bless him. The point I am making here is that if you don't know what your distractions are, you can't recognise when you are drifting and you may go too far and past the point of no return.

Here are some things to consider which can help you develop your self-awareness in this context:

1. **Track distractions for a week:** Notice what pulls your attention most often.
2. **Use reflection prompts:** Why am I struggling to focus right now? What do I need to adjust?
3. **Experiment with different focus techniques:** Find what works for you instead of forcing rigid systems. Music on, music off, lights on, lights off, and so on.

Self-awareness is a big topic, but a crucial skill to develop which can be utilised in both work and your personal life. It's an important one to invest time in.

Task management

One of the biggest derailers of focus is poor task structure. If you sit down without a plan, your brain doesn't know where to start, leading to procrastination and more doom scrolling on social media, although that cat who sounds like an old lady from the deep south is hilarious. Yes, I did just reach for my phone, but I was good and didn't look.

Having a sense of where you are going is important. I don't mean in life, but that helps as well. In this context, we're talking about the task you are working on. We can waste a lot of mental energy if we start something with no clear direction of what we want the end point to be. Some people won't need to think about this, and can just jump into a task and get to the end, making it up on the fly, but many people can't.

If task management is something you struggle with, here are some things to consider:

1. **Always outline a task before diving in:** Write the goal and small steps. Don't eat the whole metaphorical cake at once. If you are easily distracted, then smaller bite-sized chunks are easier to manage.
2. **Use structured time blocks:** Decide in advance what you'll focus on and for how long. Use the timer on your phone and then put it away from you, and just get your head down. Try ten minutes and build up.
3. **Group similar tasks together:** This stops you mentally switching too often. This could be bundling administrative tasks together. Whatever works with your job and is within your control.

Digital tools are aplenty and can streamline task management processes, as can AI tools. They are not as scary as you may think and are great for creating efficiency. You just need to learn how to use them, but they can help just prompt some thoughts on how to structure a task. Give it a whirl, if you're technologically minded. If not, then buy a shiny new notebook. I insist you reward yourself for reading my ramblings with some fabulous stationery.

Discipline

Ugh, flashback to horrendous teachers at school, but we won't get into that now. What I mean by discipline here is that focus is a skill you need to develop. Think of it like a muscle. The more you train your focus skill, the stronger it will become. And how do you keep training something to strengthen it? You got it – discipline!

If we are disciplined in our approach to developing our focus skills, it will make sustained attention easier. Do this in your preferred environment, and then bring in distractions and see if you can still be as productive. If it doesn't work the first time, keep going. It's by taking a disciplined approach that something becomes a habit or second nature to us.

Here are some tips on how to develop your discipline skill:

1. **Train with short focus sessions:** I mentioned this before regarding task management, and it works here as well. The discipline is about not being distracted in that dedicated focus time.
2. **Use your diary to block out focus time:** Some company cultures are respectful of this, and others aren't. I will put my focus time in small blocks, and mark it as private so nobody

knows what it is, and the time is short enough that people work around it. If you have a micromanaging boss who will question what your private appointment is, then this might not work for you. And also – start looking for a new job. Ain't nobody got time for that!

3. **Practise delaying distractions:** If tempted to scroll on your phone, wait five minutes first before indulging. Easier said than done, but if you reach for that expensive brick of distraction, slap yourself on the hand and give it a few more minutes before you reward yourself with cat memes and thirst traps.

Hyper-focus isn't just about removing distractions. It's about strengthening the mental skills that make deep work easier. By building self-awareness, improving task management and reinforcing discipline, you create the ideal foundation for mastering the superpower of Focus Beam.

So if DOPE feels difficult at first, start here. Focus gets stronger with practice, and every minor improvement makes a difference.

Action

Try this four-step exercise to design the perfect hyper-focus environment:

1. **Audit your distractions:** Spend a week tracking what constantly pulls you away from focus. Notifications? Background noise? Your own thoughts? Identify your biggest saboteurs and plan how to eliminate them next time.
2. **Optimise your workspace:** Take five minutes to declutter your work area every morning for a week. Gather everything you need before starting a task so you don't waste time searching for missing documents, cables, or your sanity.
3. **Experiment with preferences:** Try different ambience set-ups. Silence, music, background noise, different lighting. See what keeps you most engaged. Your ideal focus environment might surprise you.
4. **Define your endgame:** Pick a reward for completing a deep-focus session. A snack, a social media break, a quick walk or even the aforementioned kale smoothie. Use it as motivation to power through.

By using the DOPE Engine, you'll harness your Focus Beam superpower, and with practice, you'll be able to better dictate when you can hyper-focus. This takes time, and practice and will not be something you master overnight. It takes a bit of trial and error, but when you can summon the superpower on demand, it will be a complete game changer for your productivity.

What's next?

First, I'm off to get that cake. Then, we'll be looking at the superpower of Vision Crafter.

Chapter 7

The Power of Vision Crafter

Before we start, let me share some important news – I got the lemon cupcake!

Now, let's look at the power of Vision Crafter, which enhances the executive function of planning and organisation. This superpower turns ideas into structured, achievable goals, rather than letting them float around aimlessly in your brain for eternity. You know that New Year's resolution many of us have about getting a six-pack? The one that's been on my list for thirty years, so it's going *really* well!

Vision Crafter is the power to actually make your goals happen, instead of leaving them as a dream in the void. The six-pack still eludes me, I won't lie, but I have achieved many a goal over the years. I published my first novel in 2013, and now I have more than a dozen out in the world under different pen names.

Have you noticed that some people seem to have an uncanny ability to structure their lives, prioritise tasks effortlessly and always know exactly what needs to happen next? They're the ones with colour-coded planners and an organised to-do list that actually gets completed. And then there's the rest of us, staring at an overwhelming pile of chaos. To be fair, I am one of those annoying people who colour codes. Colleagues have told me that my diary is *so pretty.* I choose to take that as a compliment, regardless of the tone they use!

This is a strong superpower of mine, but I am not perfect. Looking down at the non-existent six-pack, I will take my serious addiction to multi-coloured Post-its instead.

For ADHDers, planning is both a blessing and a nightmare. We love the concept of organisation, but our execution? Questionable, at best. Who else has fifteen notebooks, a hundred productivity apps and yet still somehow forgets deadlines? Or better yet, you start five new projects before finishing the first one, convincing yourself that this time will be different. Spoiler alert: it never is! So, how do you master this superpower when your brain thrives on chaos?

Well, it's not just about forcing yourself to be organised, because, frankly, that won't work. Instead, Vision Crafter is about learning how to structure tasks in a way that works for your brain. Some people plan weeks ahead, while others need daily check-ins to stay on track. Some work best with detailed spreadsheets, while others prefer scribbling notes on random scraps of paper. The trick is finding the planning system that matches your thinking style, rather than trying to copy someone else's perfectly structured approach. I have had countless conversations with managers, telling them to stop enforcing their flawless planning system on their teams. It is flawless to you, and you only. However, let's not discount multicoloured Post-its yet, because they just might be the magic potion to mastering this superpower.

The benefits of Vision Crafter

Mastering Vision Crafter can completely change the way you work, plan and execute tasks. Sound planning and organisation aren't just about getting things done. It's about getting them done well, efficiently, and without feeling like you're constantly firefighting. Here's why Vision Crafter will revolutionise how you approach your work:

1. **Greater clarity and control:** Knowing exactly what needs to be done, how to do it and when to start, eliminates the constant nagging voice in your head. No, not your significant other. That voice which keeps saying you've forgotten something. Become a master of Vision Crafter and you'll never doubt yourself again.

2. **Smoother task execution:** When things are properly structured, tasks actually get finished rather than abandoned mid-way, when something shinier appears which grabs our attention. With Vision Crafter, you can stay on task, and save the shiny thing for later.
3. **Fewer missed deadlines:** Let's be honest, some of us only acknowledge deadlines when they start screaming at us, or our manager does. Vision Crafter helps anticipate deadlines before they turn into a crisis, reducing the inevitable panic-driven productivity burst at the last minute. Although, to be fair, I am uber-spectacular at doing something last minute, but it is stressful as f ... fiddlesticks!
4. **Reduced overwhelm:** Without structure, tasks pile up and everything feels impossible. Planning means workloads are balanced, making work manageable rather than mentally exhausting. Sounds good doesn't it? The ADHD brain can become very overwhelmed. This has helped me out so much in my life and career, and being older means I give zero fiddlesticks if someone around me is disorganised. 'Sounds like a you problem' would be my Teams status message some days, but that would probably be frowned upon.
5. **Stronger leadership and reliability:** People who can create structured plans and execute

them efficiently are trusted by teams, managers, and clients. Vision Crafter builds credibility and establishes you as a trusted pair of hands, but be careful, people like to take advantage of this rare skill set. Make sure there is something in it for you, because you know – balance is important.

People who master Vision Crafter stop feeling like they could drop from a heart attack any second because they no longer live in a permanent state of panic. Stress levels drop and productivity soars. Sounds good? But, and you knew that was coming, what happens if you don't develop this superpower?

The drawbacks of not having Vision Crafter

If planning and organisation aren't your strengths, life can quickly descend into chaos. Tasks pile up, deadlines sneak past unnoticed and projects are abandoned mid-way in favour of something more exciting, or just less overwhelming. Show of hands for who has ever started something with the best intentions, only to forget about it entirely by week two? Do not mention the six-pack thing. We are talking about you here. Let's look at the price of poor planning, because without Vision Crafter in your toolkit, things can get messy, fast:

1. **Constant firefighting:** Every task feels like a last-minute emergency, because there was no structured plan in place. If life is a series of

rushed deadlines and frantic catch-ups, chances are this is a development area for you. Or, you could just have a really chaotic manager who sits on something for three weeks, and then tells you the deadline is today, and expects you to pull something out of your a ... thin air. Not that I'm talking from personal experience or anything.

2. **Abandoned projects:** Ever had a brilliant idea and just had to get started right away? Then, something derailed you? Rather than go back to the project, you started something else? They say everyone has a book in them, but why are so many people unpublished? There could be many reasons, and frankly, I'm grateful for less competition, but I bet many of those unwritten books are down to poor planning and they could be amazing.
3. **Deadline panic:** Instead of being prepared ahead of time, you realise something is due today, and now you're scrambling to complete it on two hours of sleep and sheer adrenaline. Ah, who was transported back to their university days reading that? I remember writing a four-thousand-word essay about Alexander the Great in an afternoon. Got a good mark as well, but it's not something I would recommend as a lifestyle choice.
4. **Mental overload:** Ever had so many unstructured tasks floating around in your head? Instead of tackling them, you just sit

there, frozen by indecision? Poor planning leads to overwhelm, making it harder to start anything at all. We ADHDers can feel overwhelmed for many reasons, and this is just one of them.

5. **Lack of trust from others:** If you regularly miss deadlines or forget commitments, people will lose confidence in your reliability. This doesn't mean you aren't capable. It just means people don't know what to expect from you, and that unpredictability can cost you opportunities. Ever wondered why the superstar in the team always gets the new opportunities? It might not be favouritism, it could just be because they are the most reliable. It could also be favouritism, but that's a whole other conversation.

Vision Crafter isn't about making your life rigid, because that is boring. It is about creating structure, so you keep moving forward without feeling you are wading through quicksand. Flashback to that scene in *The NeverEnding Story*. That broke me as a kid. It must be forty years since I saw that film, and I still shed a tear thinking about it. Anyway, let's not get distracted again. It's time to look at how Vision Crafter and ADHD can be besties or mortal enemies, depending on your approach.

ADHD and Vision Crafter

For those with ADHD, planning and organisation aren't just about writing things down and hoping for the best. Structure doesn't come naturally, and the executive function responsible for keeping everything in order is often prone to chaos, avoidance and last-minute panic mode.

Have you ever sat there knowing exactly what needs to be done, but you're somehow unable to start? Oh, how I love a YouTube wormhole. The ADHD brain can get stuck at the starting line. It's often that impetus to just start something which defeats us. ADHDers love a good productivity system, but sometimes we spend more time planning than actually doing anything on the list. Anyone got a list of their lists? I'm not saying anything.

ADHD brains love the idea of a flawless execution, which sounds wonderful but, in practice, it can lead to decision paralysis. This can mean we'd rather not start at all than risk doing it wrong. Vision Crafter is about progress, not perfection, because as I've said before, that doesn't exist. However, convincing ourselves of that is much harder than it sounds.

Planning and organisation aren't about forcing rigid structure onto an ADHD brain. It's about designing systems that actually work for how our minds operate. So what's the cheat code for harnessing the power of Vision Crafter? I give you the Colour Codex.

The Colour Codex

Instead of relying on static to-do lists, the Colour Codex uses coloured Post-its, or digital colour tagging if that's more your thing, to map out tasks in a way that works well for ADHD minds. Many ADHD people are visual individuals, so it plays to our preferences. I chose the colours purely because they are the four which you get in a multi-pack of Post-its. This is a tried and tested approach which works excellently as a visual tool.

Each colour represents a different function, allowing you to categorise work with no need to overthink it.

Here's how it works:

Pink = Priority: what needs immediate attention?

Pink is the colour of urgency, well it is in this case, because there is no red in a multi-pack and P is for Priority, so even if you switched to red on a digital solution, the code would be off, so stick with these colours. Some things don't need to be messed with. Pink represents tasks you need to action first, as they carry serious consequences if ignored.

Use pink Post-its for:

1. Urgent deadlines that cannot wait.
2. High-impact tasks that directly affect goals or responsibilities.

3. Anything time-sensitive that must be done ASAP.

If a task is pink, it means: Do it first. No excuses.

Orange = Order: what needs to happen first?

Orange is the sequencing colour. It ensures you don't start step five when step one isn't done yet. We will often put something off because it is too overwhelming. This is where Orange comes in. Let's break those chunky things down into manageable pieces.

Use orange Post-its for:

1. Tasks that have dependencies. Things that must happen before other steps.
2. Processes that need a specific order to be completed properly.
3. Supporting work that helps push the bigger goal forward.

If a task is orange, it means: Put this in the right sequence. Don't skip ahead.

Green = Go: what needs to be done?

Green is your action colour. It's for tasks that aren't necessarily urgent but still need completing. This should be most of the colour you see on your board, or wherever you are putting all these Post-its. They are your core tasks that don't become urgent unless you ignore them.

Use green Post-its for:

1. Daily or weekly tasks that require steady progress.
2. Periodic tasks that can creep up on you, such as the monthly dashboard which nobody looks at. I'm sure that's not just me.
3. Work that isn't time-sensitive but must still be tackled.

If a task is green, it means: move forward and get it done, so it doesn't turn pink!

Blue = Buffer: what needs to stay visible until it's ready?

Blue is for ongoing or waiting tasks. Things that aren't urgent but can't be forgotten. ADHD brains forget tasks exist unless they're visually present, so blue Post-its serve as a visual reminder that you'll need to do something about it at some point.

Use blue Post-its for:

1. Tasks that are in progress. They are not time critical, but they are not finished yet.
2. Work that is waiting for input from others before moving forward.
3. Ideas, projects, or commitments that need attention later, but not right now.

If a task is blue, it means: keep this visible, so it doesn't fade into the background.

Why the Colour Codex works

First, I would like to thank Spencer Silver and Art Fry for the invention of the Post-it note. None of this would have been possible without you. There's a random bit of trivia for you. Might come in handy for a pub quiz, and if you have an ADHD brain, you'll remember that inane fact for all of eternity, because you don't need to.

Planning and organisation don't magically happen just because you write a to-do list and hope for the best. ADHD brains need visual prompts and that's exactly what the Colour Codex does.

Instead of staring at an overwhelming mountain of tasks, deadlines, and forgotten responsibilities, this approach makes everything visible, structured and manageable, without feeling restrictive.

I've spent far too long drowning in forgotten projects, half-baked ideas and vague plans that never actually become reality. But the Colour Codex? It turns mental clutter into something tangible. Plus, let's be honest, colour-coded Post-its just look incredibly satisfying.

Of course, if Post-its aren't your thing, there is no judgement, well maybe a bit, but digital solutions work just as well, or so I am told. Calendar tags, coloured task lists, even a very committed use of highlighters, whatever keeps your tasks structured, visible, and easy to manage.

For me, I'll be sticking with Post-its. Nothing quite beats physically moving a task from the wall to the bin once it's done. Pure dopamine hit - yes, please!

Colour Codex? I don't even know where to start

Not everyone will jump into a structured planning system. Some people will struggle more with mapping out priorities, structuring their workflow or knowing where to start. And that's okay. Vision Crafter is easier for some than it is for others.

People see me scribbling down plans, colour-coding tasks and structuring my week like I moonlight as a military strategist, but there was a time when I worked in the public sector and was only allowed dull yellow Post-its. That was a dark time. Planning takes practice, trial-and-error and utilising some of your core skills will give you the foundations you need to develop the Vision Crafter superpower.

To get you prepped to become a master of Vision Crafter, you need three essential skills: mental clarity, structured thinking and self-management.

Mental clarity

Ever sat down to work but realised you do not know what you're supposed to be doing? That's me most Monday mornings, but then I pull out the to-do list I wrote at the end of the week before and everything feels less stressful. I know what I'm supposed to be doing. The caffeine helps as well.

Here are some things to consider which can help you develop your mental clarity in this context:

1. **Have clear goals:** This ensures you don't waste time on random tasks that don't matter.
2. **Know the result:** Helps you break things down logically, rather than feeling overwhelmed by a vague idea.
3. **Clarity stops procrastination:** When you know what needs to happen, you can start getting it done, instead of spiralling into avoidance mode.

Now I know that sounds a lot easier than it is to do in practice. Sometimes you can struggle to come up with one goal, and others have too many goals. Here are some things you can do:

1. **Before working on anything, define the desired outcome:** What do I want to achieve? What does success look like? Really think about these questions. Focus on the emotions if that helps. What do you want to be thinking, feeling and doing? This is often a question I ask when career coaching, instead of people being focused on an arbitrary job title.

2. **Write a one-sentence summary of the goal before mapping any tasks:** Make it ridiculously simple. If you can't sum it up in one sentence, it's probably too vague. Get to the point: publish this book by the end of the year. See what I did there?
3. **Learn to separate high-impact tasks from time-fillers:** Not everything deserves your attention. Some things are the aforementioned pointless busy work. I will scream if I have to present my data dashboard in yet another format this month, but I digress.

If you struggle with this one, it can help to have a safe space to talk through what's going on. This could be a therapist, coach, mentor or even a friend who won't try to tell you what to do. Sometimes, we just need to talk it through, out loud, and we come to that eureka moment all by ourselves.

Structured thinking

Planning fails spectacularly when tasks are too broad, too vague, or too scattered. Vision Crafter is about structure, meaning tasks need to be sequenced logically instead of thrown together randomly. To be fair, I have achieved some great things which started from randomness, but that isn't as successful in the workplace because you can come across as disorganised.

Here are some things to consider with structured thinking:

1. **Breaking down tasks into smaller steps makes execution easier:** If you start with a gigantic, overwhelming goal, you'll never get started. There is a psychology in this. Think about weight loss. You have a goal weight and it seems so far away, but what about setting an achievable goal like five pounds? Get to that and then set another.
2. **Doing things in a logical order doesn't mean you rinse and repeat:** Apply logic to the task at hand. For example, I will write the final chapter of this book last, because it needs to pull everything together. However, for a fiction trilogy I published, I wrote a draft of the epilogue for book three before I started writing book one. This gave me an end point to work towards. Look at each task individually; just because something worked before, doesn't mean it's right to use again.
3. **Knowing what the dependencies are prevents bottlenecks:** This could be caused by the task, or by other people. I know some bosses love data and details, and will want things in a certain way, so I structure my request to appeal to their style, and then flip it for someone else. Knowing your audience means you can better flex how you present your idea to get the answer you want.

There are different approaches you can take to developing this skill, and context is important here. If you are in control of the what, why and how, then the steps below will work, but if that's down to someone else, you'll need to adapt your approach so you meet their needs. Annoying, I know, but that's managers for you. And I say this as someone who has been one for many years.

1. **Use a simple 'next step' method:** Instead of saying, 'Complete the project', ask, 'What's the next step I need to take?'
2. **Create simple visual timelines:** Even if it's just on a piece of paper, or, you guessed it, Post-its!
3. **Batch similar tasks together:** An admin blitz, then a creative focus block and so on. This will stop you switching around all the time and getting overwhelmed or burnt out.

With structured thinking, you need to always be considerate of your audience. If you meet their needs, then you can get what you want. This is referred to as the 'So what?' test. It's what you don't want the other person to say when you present your idea. Not great for us ADHDers who have major rejection sensitivity issues, so considering this in advance can help mitigate the probability of that outcome.

Self-management

Vision Crafter is useless if you make rigid plans you can't actually stick to. Planning needs to work with your brain, your pace and your natural workflow, not just look good on paper, no matter how pretty those Post-its look. I am looking at my whiteboards now. Yes, I have more than one. Don't judge me. They look stunning, but I also just realised there are thirty-five Post-its on there, and this is for tasks to complete in the next month. Not work-related. This is all personal stuff. Yes, thirty-five divides by five, but I asked you not to judge me. So, here's how self-management links to Vision Crafter:

1. **Personal systems make planning sustainable:** As mentioned, one-size-fits-all methods don't work, but you need some core principles which can apply in any situation. Ahem – Colour Codex anyone?
2. **Keeping things manageable prevents planning fatigue:** If we overcomplicate things, it leads to us giving up and we ADHDers do like to overthink things, just a tad. Remember to KISS it. Yes, you read that right. KISS stands for: keep it short and simple. Yes, my brain went there as well the first time I heard it.
3. **Expect the unexpected:** You can be the most meticulous planner in the world, but you need to develop comfort with curve balls,

because life is a bitch and it likes to give you an occasional slap. It's how we respond to it that's still within our power.

With self-management, here are some things you can do to develop the skill:

1. **Test different planning tools:** Find what sticks. Don't force a system that feels unnatural.
2. **Schedule planning moments:** Don't just assume it will happen magically. Some people need daily check-ins, others prefer weekly reviews.
3. **Accept that not every plan will work perfectly:** Plans fail sometimes, just adjust and try again. Life is all about learning from our mistakes, even if that setback hurts us at first.

Structured planning isn't about being overly rigid. It's about creating an environment where tasks flow naturally. Before jumping into the Colour Codex, mastering mental clarity, structured thinking and self-management will make planning far easier and more intuitive.

Action

I have convinced myself that colour-coded Post-its hold the key to productivity mastery. But now, it's over to you. Of course, there is only one option for the action in this chapter. You need to have a go at using the Colour Codex, so order those Post-its and get ready for some fun:

1. **Sort your priorities (Pink Post-its):** List your top-priority tasks for the next week. Let's start small. What has serious consequences if ignored? What needs your focus first? Stick those tasks on pink notes and let them guide where your energy goes.
2. **Sequence your task execution (Orange Post-its):** Identify tasks that need to happen in a specific order. What must be done before something else? What's blocking progress because another step isn't finished yet? Use orange Post-its to map out dependencies, ensuring you tackle things in the right sequence.
3. **Get moving (Green Post-its):** Write tasks that require active execution but aren't necessarily urgent. These are the next things you need to work on but don't have immediate deadlines, or a manager, breathing down your neck.
4. **Keep important tasks visible (Blue Post-its):** Some things aren't urgent right now, but if you forget them, you'll regret it later. Use blue Post-its for ongoing projects, ideas and tasks waiting on external input. Place them somewhere you'll see them regularly, so nothing disappears into the abyss, like a

whiteboard. Come on, I know you're itching to buy that whiteboard.

By using the Colour Codex, you'll start structuring your tasks without feeling trapped in overwhelming lists or rigid systems. With practice, planning stops being something you struggle with and starts feeling intuitive, like second nature.

What's next?

Now, I need to step away from this Post-it obsession before I start hoarding stationery. Next, we'll be diving into the superpower of Time Warp and exploring the elements. It will all make sense in the next chapter.

Chapter 8

The Power of Time Warp

ADHD or not, time management training is still in high demand. Although, when I've coached people on this, it is often something else, such as planning, assertiveness or self-awareness. A lot of things get clubbed into 'time management' skills, when it's not as broad as people think. I have the same with 'She needs communication skills', which is a favourite for managers. After a few follow-up questions, you discover it's influencing, assertiveness, or presenting. Much narrower and easier to develop than something all-encompassing. If only managers asked their team members these questions, their lives would be so much easier.

Time Warp is the ability to perceive time accurately, allocate it wisely and optimise how it's used. In short, it's your internal clock, the executive function that dictates whether you sail smoothly through tasks or feel like time itself has betrayed you.

As I mentioned before, prioritisation is about choosing what needs to be done first, but Time Warp? That's about understanding how long things take and planning accordingly. Pulling a random number out of the air in order to impress our boss, or to get one up on a colleague who is infuriatingly efficient, rarely ends well for us.

Some people seem to pace themselves without breaking a sweat, and meet deadlines like they are nothing. Then there is the flip side where a 'quick task' takes the entire morning. Deadlines creep up on us like Jason Vorhees in *Friday the 13th* and our use of expletives increases exponentially when we realise 'tomorrow' is actually here!

If mastering Time Warp is causing you to raise an eyebrow at me like I'm crazy, I'm going to give you a cheat code I have used with everyone, from graduates to senior executives. There are a gazillion time management models out there, and many have their merits. However, when I found I couldn't get one to fit my quirky brain, I made up my own, and it's awesome – yes, I did just say that!

The benefits of Time Warp

When time management is a superpower rather than a struggle, life feels far less chaotic. Deadlines are met without the stress-induced adrenaline rush, meaning no more frantic typing at midnight while promising yourself this will never happen again. Here are five benefits of developing the Time Warp superpower:

1. **You take control, not your calendar:** Instead of reacting to looming deadlines and constantly fighting last-minute chaos, you plan your time with intention. Sounds too good to be true, doesn't it? Time Warp gives you the ability to lead your day rather than chasing it, screaming for more time.
2. **Clarity replaces panic:** When your time is structured, decisions become clearer and less emotionally charged. You can step back, assess priorities objectively and respond with purpose, not adrenaline-fuelled guesswork keeping you awake in the early hours of the morning. You know when you keep looking at the clock and counting down how little sleep you are now going to get?
3. **Procrastination loses its grip:** One of Time Warp's stealthiest strengths? It breaks the loop of avoid–delay–panic–scramble. With better time awareness and structure, you're far more likely to start a task in good time, work steadily and finish with breathing room. You're not just getting it done, you're completing it without the internal chaos. Beating the procrastination monster will have a ripple effect on other ADHD superpowers.
4. **Reputation glow-up:** People who manage their time well are dependable, organised and

professional because, let's be real, they are. Once you harness Time Warp, everyone looks at you differently. They trust you to deliver. You're a reliable pair of hands. Yes, some people will take the proverbial with that and give you too much. But someone who delivers on their promises has a strong reputation within any business.

5. **More time to recharge your batteries:** Each day we complete tasks or have interactions with others which deplete our energy, and we all have a different fuel which tops us back up. I'm not talking about coffee. Writing is big for me. I can write ten thousand words and have more energy than when I started. You'll have your own thing. It's important to use the time capacity you've created to do something meaningful which will replenish your energy stores. Whether it's family, friends, hobbies or a much-needed rest, you finally get to enjoy life beyond the to-do list, guilt-free and on your own terms.

With Time Warp, decision-making becomes clearer, because time is planned with intention rather than dictated by urgency. Instead of reacting under pressure, you can actually weigh up options objectively and make better choices. Productivity increases when time is used deliberately, instead of being lost in distractions and procrastination rabbit holes. It also doesn't hurt that people who consistently meet deadlines and manage their workload effectively are reliable, competent and highly trustworthy. So, what's the flip side?

The drawbacks of not having Time Warp

Without Time Warp, time becomes a fickle, unreliable thing, constantly slipping through your fingers, leaving you scrambling to meet deadlines that seemed eons in the future just yesterday. A task stretches far beyond its expected timeframe, convincing you it'll take 'five minutes', only for it to consume an entire day or more. Here are five drawbacks to not developing this superpower:

1. **Perpetual crisis mode:** When time isn't managed well, nearly everything turns into an emergency. Tasks pile until they're urgent, deadlines sneak attack you at the worst moments and you live in a loop of stress-fuelled scrambling. Some people thrive in this permanent state of chaos and panic, and I have found it effective in getting things done, but it's not a healthy space to occupy all the time.
2. **Decision-making impairment:** Without time awareness, choices are often rushed, emotionally charged, or delayed until you are forced to take action. That might come from an email from your boss which says, 'Just following up', which is beautifully passive-aggressive. What happens without Time Warp

is you end up reacting to the most urgent demand rather than making thoughtful, intentional decisions, leading to missed opportunities or unnecessary mistakes.

3. **Procrastination becomes a lifestyle:** Without this superpower, procrastination isn't just a habit, it becomes your default setting. You may even convince yourself you 'work better under pressure', which is just your adrenaline speaking, not a logical strategy. Excess pressure leads to stress, which leads to burnout and other mental health concerns. It's not worth it in the long run.
4. **Reputational impact:** Inconsistency in time management can affect how others see you. Missed deadlines, last-minute rushes or forgetfulness can lead to people perceiving you as disorganised or unreliable, even when you're working incredibly hard behind the scenes. Remember, effort isn't always visible, but outcomes are. One job I have a lot of empathy for is event managers. Nobody thinks twice about all the work that has gone into an event which runs smoothly, but they certainly have something to say if anything goes wrong. Round of applause for all the event managers who have to deal with idiots every day.
5. **Important things always come last:** When you're constantly reacting, you rarely get to the things that matter most, such as rest,

> relationships, creativity or long-term goals. Life becomes about keeping up, and you're in this cycle of saying, 'I'll start on Monday.' Over time, that takes a toll on both confidence and wellbeing.

Time Warp isn't about working faster, it's about working smarter. Without it, time isn't something you control, it's something that betrays you at every turn.

ADHD and Time Warp

For those with ADHD, time isn't a straightforward concept. It's more like a vague suggestion rather than a measurable reality. Time management is one of the biggest executive function struggles, not because tasks are inherently difficult, but because time itself rarely feels real. Some days, five minutes feels like an hour, and other days, an entire afternoon vanishes in what seems like seconds.

ADHD brains experience time blindness, making it difficult to accurately judge how long tasks should take. What seems like a quick job somehow drags out endlessly, while urgent deadlines sneak up faster than expected, leading to panic-mode productivity sprints. Hyper-focus can also distort time, causing people to lock into a task for hours without realising that everything else has been neglected. This can be great for deep work, but devastating for balanced productivity, because while the task at hand may progress, everything else is crumbling in the background.

Because ADHD brains love an adrenaline rush, they often rely on urgency to force productivity. Deadlines become the trigger for action. If something isn't urgent, it often gets pushed aside indefinitely, because without that external pressure, it simply doesn't feel important enough to engage with. Then there's distracted time loss, where a five-minute break turns into an hour, and a quick email check spirals into a Wikipedia rabbit hole. Who was the King of England in 1263? Who cares! (It was Henry III, because I know you were thinking of looking it up.)

The ADHD brain isn't wired for traditional time tracking, which is why Time Warp must be built intentionally. Rather than relying on instinct, ADHD time management works best when time is made visible, structured and predictable because, left unchecked, time will absolutely betray you.

The Element Compass

ADHD time management doesn't work with one-size-fits-all solutions. Some people thrive on structure, while others crash and burn at the mere thought of a rigid schedule. That's where the Element Compass comes in. I called it a compass because it gives direction. I know that's obvious, but I have been asked that question too many times, so I'm getting that one out of the way.

This is a strategy that categorises people by their natural productivity rhythm, allowing them to use time effectively in a way that best works for their brain. Before we get into how to use this to your advantage, let's break down the four elements: earth, fire, wind and rain.

Earth: the structured planner

Earth types love clarity, routine, and predictability. They function best with fixed schedules, knowing exactly what's happening next and how long it will take. If time feels clear and structured, they can pace themselves efficiently and avoid last-minute chaos.

Fire: the late starter, intense finisher

Fire types struggle to get moving in the morning, but hit peak productivity later in the day. They hyper-focus deeply, working in intense bursts of energy, often getting more done in the afternoon or evening than they ever could in a morning.

Wind: the chaotic executor

Wind types do not work in structured patterns. Their productivity is unpredictable, and they thrive in flexible, ever-changing environments. These individuals jump between tasks impulsively, yet still somehow get everything done in their own chaotic way.

Rain: the short-burst worker

Rain types cannot sustain long focus periods, but work brilliantly in short, structured chunks. They burn out fast, so their ideal rhythm involves frequent, intentional breaks to reset energy levels.

How to identify your element

Before using this cheat code, you need to know where you naturally fit. Here are three questions to ask yourself:

1. ***When are you most productive?***
   a. Morning.
   b. Afternoon/evening.
   c. Completely random moments with no consistency.
   d. Quick bursts throughout the day.
2. ***What happens when you try to stick to a schedule?***
   a. You thrive with a well-structured plan.
   b. You procrastinate all morning, then suddenly get everything done in one go.
   c. You completely ignore schedules and work whenever it feels right.
   d. You burn out quickly if focus sessions are too long.
3. ***What's your biggest productivity struggle?***
   a. Feeling overwhelmed without a coherent plan.

b. Wasting half the day before finally kicking into gear.
c. Avoiding structure entirely and working unpredictably.
d. Fatigue from long work sessions, needing breaks to stay functional.

If you answered mostly A, then you identify more with Earth. B is Fire, C is Wind and D is Rain. If you have a mix, then keep an open mind as we continue to explore the cheat code and one may resonate more than the other.

Using the Element Compass

Let's talk about how to use this effectively. Remember, this isn't about forcing yourself into rigid planning, it's about working with your strengths to master Time Warp.

Earth

Since you operate best with structured time, focus on pacing yourself efficiently so you don't burn out too early. Break large tasks into scheduled blocks, so you are less likely to lose track of time by being sucked into deep work. Create a check-in on progress, which could be something as simple as an alert on your phone. This will give you a moment to pause and determine if you are allocating the right time to things.

Fire

Your peak productivity is in the afternoon so use that to your advantage. Front-load simple tasks in the morning so you don't waste energy. This could be decluttering emails, admin and anything else which involves little brain power. Schedule deep work for later in the day. If you don't have control over when you complete tasks, talk to your manager and see if anything can be done to flex things around to accommodate your working style. If you don't ask, you'll never know.

Wind

Since structured schedules aren't your thing, use a flexible system. Allow yourself variety to switch between tasks without guilt as long you keep making progress. Use priority lists instead of rigid schedules, making sure important tasks don't get lost in the chaos. I have to say it again, but Post-its work really well here. Sticking them to the bottom of your screen is a constant visual reminder that certain things need to get done today.

Rain

Since long focus periods don't suit you, use shorter, high-intensity sessions followed by intentional breaks. The Pomodoro Technique will be a good one for you to consider. You work in a twenty-five-minute sprint and then have a break for five minutes. Discipline is important for this one, so set small, clear goals for each focus sprint, and don't get distracted by the bigger task.

Not ready for the Element Compass?

Not everyone is going to immediately master Time Warp. Some people will struggle with tracking time, others will completely underestimate how long things take, and some will just stare blankly at their schedule, wondering where the last five hours went. That's normal. Time Warp isn't built in a day.

So, if time management feels like a lost cause right now, don't panic. Developing foundational skills can make time feel less like an unpredictable force of nature and more like something you can control.

To get started, let's cover three core skills that will make mastering Time Warp far easier: time tracking, pace perception, and structured flexibility.

Time tracking

Ever sat down to work, looked up two hours later and thought, 'What just happened?' Time disappears faster than expected, and most people do not know where it actually goes. This is why tracking your time usage is important:

1. **Awareness of what time of day it is:** If you don't track time properly, you'll always feel like it vanishes without warning. Have it in-your-face visible, which could be a clock on the wall, or a digital one on your desk.

2. **Understanding your own time patterns:** This helps identify where time loss happens, whether that's distractions, overestimating how long something will take or falling into hyper-focus traps.
3. **Time tracking allows you to catch inefficiencies**: Having this awareness means you can act before they derail productivity, rather than looking back and wondering where the entire day went.

That all sounds great, doesn't it? But I can guess you are probably thinking, 'Well, that's easy for him to say,' and I get that. This is easier for some than it is for others, and it can be a bigger challenge for people with ADHD. Here are some pointers:

1. **Run a time audit for a week:** Track how long tasks actually take compared to what you *think* they take. Yes, that will be a revelation.
2. **Use timers to check in on progress every hour:** Not to pressure yourself, but to see whether time is being spent effectively or just evaporating.
3. **Write a summary at the end of each day:** A quick note of what got done, what took too long and what completely slipped your mind.

Pace prediction

ADHD brains are notoriously bad at predicting task length. What should take ten minutes somehow turns into an hour, and what seems like a gigantic project actually isn't that bad once you start. Here is why learning to estimate time correctly is a fundamental skill:

1. **Proper pace prediction prevents task overload:** Knowing what's realistic rather than setting impossible goals. This is not to stop you setting yourself stretch targets. This is about that daily grind, not your hopes and dreams. You should always go big with those.
2. **Understanding how long things actually take:** This stops you from scheduling four hours' worth of work into a ninety-minute window. We've all been there, especially when the big boss comes along and asks you to do something. Wanting to impress them, you do it in a nanosecond, when they never asked for it that quickly. But, next time, they will.
3. **Knowing your own speed for different tasks:** This means you are not always rushing at the last minute. Some tasks take me five minutes if my energy levels are high but, if they are low, then an 'End of the week' response typically means I overdeliver, which is never a bad thing to be known for.

Again, I know that all sounds easier said than done, so here are some tips on how you can develop your pace prediction skills:

1. **Start using a time prediction method:** Before you begin a task, guess how long it will take, then track the actual result. This will be wildly inaccurate at first, but improves with practice.
2. **Compare similar past tasks:** Look back at how long similar work has taken before, and use that information to build more realistic expectations.
3. **Create buffer zones in your schedule:** If you *think* something takes an hour, schedule ninety minutes instead, allowing for unexpected delays. Assume the working day is six hours, instead of eight, so you've got buffer time for when other people's time blindness affects you, such as your, ahem ... manager. If anyone asks, I'll deny I ever said such a thing.

Structured flexibility

The Time Warp superpower isn't about rigid scheduling. It's about knowing how to adjust without losing control. That's where the skill of structured flexibility can help. When unexpected things happen, time management could collapse entirely. The skill of structured flexibility has some critical benefits for efficiency:

1. **Knowing the rigidity of different tasks:** Some tasks must be done at set times, but many can shift around when needed. Knowing which is which prevents chaos. Just because your boss sent you an email, doesn't mean they are expecting an immediate response, unless they are one of those who call you straight after sending said email. If that is the case ... run!
2. **Flexibility allows you to adapt:** When tasks take longer than expected, rather than having your schedule fall apart over one delay. Things outside our control can cause these delays. Something which is urgent to us, might not be to someone else. Ever heard, 'Your poor planning does not constitute my emergency?' With structured flexibility you'll be more adaptive to people being disorganised and generally irritating.
3. **Efficiency without pressure:** Not everything has to be hyper-planned, but nothing should be entirely random. Don't add things to your to do list until they have been considered. You can always have a separate list to collate things as they come up, and you can look at them when you're not under pressure.

But how do we do this? It all sounds simple, but the reality is very different when our brains run at a million miles an hour. Here are some things you can try:

1. **Label tasks as 'fixed' or 'flexible':** Some things must happen on schedule, while others can be moved around without consequence. Challenge yourself when doing this. As a general rule, most tasks should be in the 'flexible' column, but it will vary for different jobs, and might not work as an approach for everyone.
2. **Use rolling time blocks:** Instead of scheduling things at precise times, allow for adjustment windows, so if a task overruns, it doesn't wreck your entire day. Again, you might not have control over your entire schedule, so work within the parameters of what you can flex.
3. **Have contingency plans:** If something gets delayed, know what can shift, so time isn't wasted stressing about disruptions. Therefore, it's important not to leave things until the last minute.

Building self-awareness, improving time estimation and mastering structured flexibility will make time management far less frustrating. Instead of fighting against time, you'll start working with it, making deadlines predictable, schedules manageable and the workload feels in control.

If time management feels impossible, start here. The more you refine these personal effectiveness skills, the easier it will be to make Time Warp work for you rather than against you.

Action

Time management isn't something you wake up one morning magically good at. It takes deliberate practice, refining the way you perceive, estimate, and structure time.

To help you take control of your Time Warp superpower, try this three-step exercise:

1. **Track perception versus reality:** For the next week, before starting a task, guess how long it will take. Then, track the actual result. How close were you? If you overestimated or underestimated, note what threw your judgement off.
2. **Identify your productivity element:** Use the Element Compass to figure out when and how you work best: Earth, Fire, Wind or Rain. Once you know your style, adjust your time planning accordingly so you're working *with* your brain instead of against it.
3. **Build your time structure:** Take what you've learned from tracking your time perception and identifying your productivity rhythm, and

experiment with new scheduling techniques. Try time blocks, buffer zones or short-focus bursts, based on what naturally fits your element.

Time Warp is about working smarter, not forcing yourself into rigid systems. The more you understand your own time patterns, the easier it will be to stay ahead of tasks rather than constantly playing catch-up.

What's next?

Next, we move on to tackling the executive function of working memory. It's the power of Mind Vault.

Chapter 9

The Power of Mind Vault

Ever had a brilliant idea vanish into thin air before you could write it down? Or completely blanked when you walked into a room? Congratulations, you've experienced the unpredictability of working memory. It's not an age thing. I've been blanking since I was old enough to talk.

Working memory isn't just about remembering facts, it's about being able to hold, manipulate and use information in real time. Imagine having a mental filing system where key details are stored, which you can recall without thinking. Sounds impossible, doesn't it? Some people seem to retain conversations, deadlines and tiny details of inane facts. Do you remember who was the King of England in 1263? No looking back!

Others? Including me. We live in a heightened sense of panic with frantic Post-its, calendar reminders and sheer luck, praying we don't forget what we were supposed to be doing five minutes ago.

For those who master Mind Vault, life feels structured instead of chaotic. There's no scrambling to recall half-finished thoughts, no frustrated searching for lost details and no blank-staring at someone who swears you agreed to something last week, but you have absolutely no memory of it. Strong working memory allows for faster decision-making and smoother execution of complex tasks.

Mind Vault isn't something you're born with or doomed to struggle with forever. It's a skill that can be developed and refined, just like with any of the other executive functions. Some people naturally excel at holding multiple pieces of information in their minds at once, while others need external tools and techniques to compensate. Neither approach is better or worse. It's just about finding what works best for your brain.

If you're someone who frequently loses track of tasks, forgets information too quickly or struggles to hold multiple details in your mind at once, don't panic. This superpower is for you.

The benefits of Mind Vault

When working memory is strong, life feels noticeably smoother. Tasks that once felt overwhelming suddenly become manageable, and recalling information no longer requires frantic searches through notes or mental gymnastics to piece together missing details. Instead of losing track of important facts mid-sentence, everything stays accessible, ready to be used exactly when needed. Conversations flow better, instructions don't slip away seconds after hearing them, including minor details, like where you left your phone – yes, I did it again. There are many benefits of developing the Mind Vault superpower, but of course, we'll stick to five:

1. **Complex tasks become easier to navigate:** Instead of juggling multiple-step processes and hoping nothing gets forgotten along the way, information sticks. This results in fewer moments of confusion, or adrenaline-fuelled panic if you're me. As a result you're more efficient, because instead of double-checking everything, you're confident in what you're delivering.
2. **Learning and problem-solving:** When the memory is doing what it should be – remembering things – information is processed faster, retained longer and applied more effectively. I can pick up when people in the training room have strong working memory, because their questions are focused on execution of the concepts I am sharing, rather than seeking constant clarification.
3. **Mental efficiency boosts productivity:** People with a strong Mind Vault superpower can keep knowledge with minimal effort and

recall important data on command. They navigate complex tasks without constant self-doubt, and just get on with delivering, as everything is stored in their brilliant brain.

4. **Credibility and trust:** The ability to hold onto critical details with no need for excessive reminders builds credibility and trust. This makes others feel confident in their ability to deliver on commitments. They are someone reliable, who doesn't need seventeen check-in calls in two weeks. This is not an exaggeration. Someone really subjected me to this. And breathe!
5. **Reduce stress and overwhelm:** No more staring blankly at an unfinished task, trying to recall what happened a few seconds ago. Getting halfway through an important point, only to forget where you were going? Those days are over if you have Mind Vault. Your memory becomes an asset, rather than that annoying colleague who has decided it's their daily mission to make you look foolish.

Mind Vault isn't about having a photographic memory or memorising everything perfectly. It's about developing the ability to store, process and recall information exactly when it's needed. Once mastered, it becomes one of the most powerful tools for productivity, efficiency and mental clarity.

The drawbacks of poor working memory

Without a well-developed Mind Vault, everything feels disjointed and unreliable. Tasks slip through the cracks, information vanishes without warning, and memory stops being dependable. Instead of moving through responsibilities with ease, every task becomes an uphill battle, requiring constant backtracking and clarifications. This can lead to self-doubt, exhaustion and burnout.

1. **Persistent forgetfulness:** Struggling to retain details means needing frequent reminders, whether that's asking colleagues to repeat instructions, checking notes multiple times or scrambling through emails for information that should have been stored mentally. This will cause people to gossip behind your back, or maybe that's just HR professionals. Either way, I'd prefer to avoid the likelihood of it happening. My overactive imagination doesn't need to be wondering what they are saying about me.
2. **Lost tasks and forgotten deadlines:** Projects rely on strong mental organisation, but without effective working memory, important steps slip through the cracks, causing errors, delays and frustration. Instead of executing tasks smoothly, work feels scattered and projects start falling apart simply because critical steps don't get

remembered in the right order. I'm sure we've all met one of those project managers before, and wonder why they still have a job. Let's make sure that isn't us.

3. **Mental exhaustion:** When memory recall isn't instant, the brain spends a large amount of energy trying to piece everything back together. Constantly retracing steps to remember instructions, deadlines or previous conversations turns productivity into a draining experience.
4. **Relationships with others:** When commitments are regularly forgotten, it creates inefficiency, forcing others to compensate for missing details or repeatedly remind you. Over time, this can damage professional credibility, making people hesitate to trust that work will be completed accurately or on time. 'It'll just be quicker to do it myself' could become a common phrase associated with someone who lacks the Mind Vault superpower.
5. **Inconsistent performance under pressure:** When your working memory falters in fast-paced or high-stakes situations, performance can plummet just when it matters most. Whether it's forgetting key points mid-presentation, losing track of multi-step processes or blanking during complex conversations, the pressure to 'hold it all together' becomes overwhelming.

To cope with poor working memory, many people rely heavily on external memory systems, such as apps, notes or constant reminders to track information. While external tools can be incredibly useful, complete dependence on them becomes a problem when systems fail. If a note isn't written, if an app doesn't send an alert or if an important detail doesn't get logged, there's no back-up, leading to missed deadlines, forgotten appointments and total confusion. Technology is a brilliant invention, and the majority of us can no longer cope without it, but the best way to recall important information when you need it is to develop the Mind Vault superpower.

ADHD and Mind Vault

With ADHD, working memory can feel less like a secure vault and more like a bucket full of holes. Does anyone remember 'There's a Hole in my Bucket' or am I showing my age here?

We can know we've got to do something important, and it's right there. We might get mildly distracted, which could be something as simple as a wandering thought, and it's gone. You return to the kitchen to trigger recall, and open the fridge. You're not sure if the prompt came from the fridge, but you're grasping at straws. And now, you want a drink, and completely forget you were going to do something. A few hours later, your better half comes home and asks, 'Did you do that thing?' Oops. You quickly rush to do it whilst feeling the death stare on the back of your neck, telling yourself you'll get flowers delivered as an apology, but you forget to do that as well.

Short-term information loss is one of the biggest obstacles ADHD brains face. Instead of holding onto details long enough to use them effectively, key facts fade quickly, requiring extra effort to keep conversations, instructions or planning on track. Ever been given directions, nodded confidently, then realised two minutes later you remember absolutely nothing? That's ADHD-working memory in action, and without reinforcement, it's a constant uphill battle.

The challenge of multi-step tasks makes completing complex processes significantly harder. Imagine following a recipe, but by the time you finish chopping the vegetables, you've already forgotten what comes next. Or tackling a work project, only to realise halfway through that you missed a crucial step because the sequence didn't stick. ADHD-working memory struggles with holding multiple details at once, meaning tasks often feel fragmented rather than seamless.

Forgetfulness doesn't just affect work. Misplacing items - yes, I lost my phone again today - forgetting appointments, or losing track of commitments become the norm. ADHD brains rarely store and retrieve details in the same way neurotypical brains do, making simple tasks surprisingly difficult to keep consistent.

Because of this constant battle against forgetfulness, many ADHD individuals overcompensate through external tools, relying heavily on notes, reminders, alarms and productivity apps to reinforce memory. While these systems can be lifesavers, they also create a dependence. If something isn't logged properly, it's gone forever. If an appointment isn't entered in a calendar, there's a high chance it won't exist when the time comes.

Following verbal instructions also presents a significant challenge. Without written prompts or visual reinforcement, information is often lost instantly, forcing constant repetition to stay on track. It can be incredibly awkward when you ask someone who they are, and they tell you you've worked together for two years. Trust me – I know!

Mastering Mind Vault isn't about forcing ADHD brains to suddenly retain information perfectly. It's about creating structured systems that reinforce memory, ensuring details stick instead of vanishing into oblivion. Relying solely on mental storage isn't always enough. You need that all important cheat code. Enter, the ECHO Index.

The ECHO Index

ADHD memory isn't just forgetful, it's sneaky. It convinces you that something is memorised, then suddenly erases it from existence without warning. The ECHO Index ensures information doesn't slip away into the void, using four essential techniques that reinforce recall without turning it into a chore.

Here's how it works:

E = Engage: Make it meaningful

Ever noticed how useless facts stick in your mind for years, but important information disappears immediately? That's because the brain doesn't easily store details unless they feel engaging or relevant. Consider the following:

1. Connect new information to emotions, stories or absurd imagery. If it's weird, your brain will keep it. Why do we always remember that presentation when someone shared their personal story over the CEO sharing the annual results?
2. Turn details into exaggerated, ridiculous associations. Need to remember someone called Julie? Picture her doing something which links to her character, which could be juggling tomatoes or reading a dirty book. I will never forget when an older, church-going colleague said *Fifty Shades of Grey* was tame. That was over a decade ago, and I can immediately recall the setting, time of day, and context of when that conversation happened.
3. Make it funny. Humour locks memories in place better than repetition ever will. I use

this approach in training. Whether it's an amusing anecdote or self-deprecating humour, it enables people to recall and retain the subject, and works well for neurodivergent and neurotypical people.

C = Chunk: Break it down

ADHD brains don't store giant blocks of information, they thrive on digestible chunks. Ever wondered why song lyrics stick so easily? It's because they use rhythm and pattern to make recall effortless.

1. Split large tasks into smaller pieces instead of dumping it all in one go. You know what can help you do this? You guessed it, Post-its! I promise I am not on commission.
2. Use short, rhythmic phrases to remember key concepts. Why do you think all these cheat codes use acronyms or are associated with something else, such as the elements? About fifteen years ago, I was at a trainer's event, and someone explained how you could use music to remember Microsoft Office shortcuts, which I can still remember.
3. Group similar details together so your brain remembers relationships, not just random facts. This could be association to a person, place, day of the week or anything you want.

H = Hear: Say it out loud

Silent thoughts slip away too easily, but verbal repetition activates deeper memory processing. Ever read something but immediately forget it, yet somehow remember things you've talked about weeks later? That's because hearing information helps lock it in better than just thinking.

1. Say key details out loud instead of just reading them. Your brain processes spoken words differently. It's why you should always practise presentations by speaking aloud. Not only does it help you retain key information so you aren't beholden to a script, you can pick up on something which doesn't work more easily or mistakes you've missed from reading.
2. Repeat critical information a few times before moving on, and do this several times. When I have to remember a six-digit code as a security measure for a website, I say the number aloud three times and I can punch it straight in.
3. Teach it to someone else. If you have to explain something to another person, it will enable memory recall, because you'll associate the memory of sharing it with the information.

O = Organise: Create a mental anchor

If information isn't stored accessibly, your brain won't know where to find it when needed. You need an element of organisation for your memory, so you can recall information when it's needed. Organisation? Yes, that dreaded word, and no, I will not use Post-its this time.

1. Assign core reference points for critical information. This could be one word, such as ECHO or DOPE. It could be a short sentence jotted down on a ... random square piece of paper, which sticks to things. See, I didn't say it again.
2. Group details under a single memorable concept. If you need to recall multiple facts, link them under one easy-to-remember keyword. I've always found it amusing when companies use terms like Project Duck when they are doing something secret, which could be anything from a disciplinary matter to a proposed acquisition. Whereas Project Duck, to me, would be a surprise birthday dinner for someone at a Chinese restaurant. And now it's eight o'clock in the morning on a Sunday and I want crispy duck. Damn my brain.
3. Use mind maps or visual memory tricks to prompt recall. I often use PowerPoint to not only present my proposals, but to set out

ideas that I might not come back to for several weeks.

Why the ECHO Index works

Instead of forcing traditional memorisation techniques, this method uses emotional connection, chunking, verbal reinforcement and structured storage to make memory recall effortless.

This is a valuable cheat code for anyone, ADHD or not. Most people forget things if there isn't a prompt to trigger recall. Instead of hoping memory works, the ECHO Index ensures information sticks by reinforcing recall in ways ADHD brains better respond to.

Not ready for the ECHO Index?

If Mind Vault feels like a disaster right now, don't panic. You're not alone. Some people naturally retain details with ease, while others live in a constant state of, 'Wait, what was I doing again?' Working memory isn't just about memorisation, it's about being able to hold and use information efficiently without constantly feeling like your brain is playing hide-and-seek with important details.

Before jumping into the ECHO Index, strengthening personal effectiveness skills can make memory recall smoother, more structured and significantly less frustrating. Let's talk about three skills that make mastering Mind Vault far easier: active recall, reflective thinking and verbal precision.

Active recall

Active recall is the art of remembering on purpose, not just hoping the right detail will magically appear mid-meeting or while you're standing in the supermarket wondering what you came in for. I've lost count of the amount of times I have come back from the shops having spent over a hundred quid, but didn't get the milk I went in for. When you practise active recall, you're strengthening the connections in your brain like muscle memory. There are significant benefits to developing this skill:

1. **Think of the brain as a library vault:** I like to imagine there are millions of filing cabinets in my brain and little people running around screaming, trying to keep up with what I am asking for. Active recall enables you to be more precise in asking your brain to help and give those poor people an easier day.
2. **Active recall trains your brain to stop being lazy at the storing stage:** When the pressure's on, it actually delivers instead of ghosting you. We've all been there.
3. **It turns memory into an actual skill you can train:** Not just a game of 'Will it come back to me before the meeting ends?' But a simple 'I'd like some time to reflect' is always a good holding response – remember that! Say it out loud three times now, so it sticks.

Active recall takes time to master, and won't always be perfect, but here are some things you can you do to strengthen the skill:

1. **Quiz yourself on new information without looking:** Try writing or saying it aloud.
2. **Create your own prompt tools:** Use flashcards, voice notes, or mini 'memory tests'.
3. **Space out your reviews:** Give your brain time to forget a little before practising recall again. This is important. Forgetting things is all part of the learning process, which sounds bizarre, but it aids recall because you don't want to feel that emotion you did when you forgot it the first time.

Reflective thinking

Reflective thinking isn't about beating yourself up when your brain blanks. It's about asking, 'Why didn't that stick?' Was it timing, stress, distraction, poor storage or just the fact you were hungry and wondering if that coleslaw would be okay for a day after its use-by date? Once you get curious about your memory slip-ups instead of frustrated, you uncover patterns and that's where real improvement happens. The skill of reflective thinking has many benefits:

1. **Turns 'I forgot' into useful feedback:** This helps you tweak how you store and retrieve information in the future, and it doesn't hurt to be honest if you are comfortable being vulnerable. It also helps to educate people that your brain works differently to others.
2. **Shift your response from frustration to curiosity:** Give memory slip-ups a role in your growth rather than just annoyance. It can be incredibly frustrating, and this isn't just something which afflicts ADHDers, but we are naturally curious, so use that to your advantage when things slip.
3. **Create a personal memory playbook:** Use past mistakes to guide smarter strategies for future recall. I've lost count of the number of companies who have a 'learn from our mistakes' mantra in their values, so why can't we take this approach as individuals?

That all sounds great, doesn't it? But how do we develop this skill? Here are some tips for you to improve your reflective thinking:

1. **Daily reflections:** At the end of each day, jot down one thing you remembered easily, and one thing you completely forgot, if you can remember it. Ask yourself what made the difference.
2. **Reflect on each memory blank:** Pause and consider what was the cause. Was it a

distraction or was the information unmemorable? This will help you develop the right strategy in the future.

3. **Practise explaining things you've learned to someone else:** If you can teach it to someone else, you'll have a stronger chance of recalling it when needed. You will need a willing volunteer who isn't too much of a subject expert on the matter. ADHDers are like magnets, we are drawn to each other, so it might be easier than you think to find a willing buddy.

Verbal precision

Clarity boosts memory. When your thoughts are vague, or full of filler, they're harder to hold onto, and even harder to recall under pressure. Verbal precision is the skill of saying what you mean, and not being vague or wishy washy. For example, the husband asked me to get him something for lunch, so I picked him up a sandwich. The one he always orders. What does he say?

'Oh, I wanted something hot.'

And breathe!

You get what I mean. By being more precise, everyone has greater clarity on the expectations. Here are some benefits of developing this skill:

1. **Sharper memory recall under pressure:** When your thoughts are filed away precisely by those little people in your brain, you can recall the memories when you need them. No more mental rummaging through the vaults and frantically scrambling through your notebook as the creeping death of your manager asking everyone for an update is getting closer to you.
2. **More impactful communication:** Whether it's a meeting, an email or explaining why something hot doesn't mean microwaving said sandwich. Yes, I made that suggestion. Simple expression helps others understand you faster, and with fewer raised eyebrows.
3. **Fewer misunderstandings and memory misfires:** The clearer you are, the less often your brain, and everyone else's, will need to play a game of mental charades trying to interpret what you actually mean.

'Did you get that thing?'

'What thing?'

'That thing?'

'WHAT THING?!'

You get what I mean. 'Thing' or 'thingy' are common words used by ADHDers, and how dare you not understand what we are referring to? So, how can you develop the skill of verbal precision?

1. **Practise summarising:** Whether it be tasks, meeting notes or instructions, in one or two punchy sentences. No waffling allowed. Consider using an AI tool to support, not replace, your notetaking. Make your own notes and compare them to the AI tool. Lean on the tool more if you need to, but don't let it become a crutch, as it won't be available in every scenario, such as the infamous 'hot lunch'.
2. **Turn vague ideas into sharp memorable phrases:** They should capture the essence of what you're trying to remember. Use a notes app to jot things down as they come to you and dedicate time to refine your thoughts into something punchy.
3. **Slow your speech when thinking aloud:** A common thing for ADHDers is our brain moves fast, so we will naturally talk at rapid speed. Try reading aloud, and do it with something which isn't familiar to you as you won't unconsciously race ahead, believing you've heard it all before.

Developing these personal effectiveness skills will give you the foundations for creating the Mind Vault superpower. It's one where I can have great days, and some not so much. I find I am better at work, rather than at home. That's probably because of consequences, but I find I am more conscious of when I need to use the superpower, which helps significantly with working memory.

Action

It should come as no surprise that the action I am going to give you for this chapter is to have a go at using the ECHO Index. Pick one actual situation in the next forty-eight hours that normally leads to a memory fail. Maybe it's forgetting meeting points, a follow-up task, names at networking events or remembering your partner asked you *again* not to leave crumbs in the butter - oops!

For this moment, use the full ECHO Index:

1. **Engage:** Make the detail memorable. Add a weird image, crack a mental joke or link it to something outrageous and NSFW.
2. **Chunk:** Break it down. What's the smallest part of this thing you actually need to remember right now?
3. **Hear:** Say it aloud. Even if it's just for your cat. She's always giving me death stares anyway. Bonus points for saying it dramatically. Pretend you are onstage, and do it when nobody else is home so you don't feel judged, other than by said cat.
4. **Organise:** Anchor it with a label. One word. One mental tag. One thing that makes it impossible to ignore. And if it helps, use a Post-it note, but just one. Sorry, but Post-its

> are part of my belief system, so you're not allowed to judge me.

Then come back to it after two days. Did it stick? What helped? What didn't? Reflect. Refine. Repeat. And keep it going. Try this for a month. Yes, you heard me right. A. Month. Studies show it takes at least ninety days to develop a habit, so I'm being generous here.

What's next?

So, that's Mind Vault done. Now, we move onto the C word. No, not that one! I am talking about: Change. Some people love it, and others not so much. But change is like death and taxes. An inevitable part of life. How do we become more adaptable? You need the superpower of Mental Morph.

Chapter 10

The Power of Mental Morph

Ever watched someone be unaffected by an enormous change to a piece of work they have spent months on, and seem excited by the new challenge? Yeah, I hate those people too. But that's a perfect example of Mental Morph in action. It's the ability to adapt, shift perspectives and embrace change without throwing a tantrum, even the internal ones we have twenty times a day at work. It's what separates the people who go with the flow from the ones clutching their carefully crafted project plans and weeping like the world has ended. I have definitely never done that!

Cognitive flexibility is the executive function that determines how well you roll with life's surprises. It's not about suppressing emotions, and presenting to the world as though you're okay with the change. Those who have the superpower of Mental Morph are actually okay with the change. Who would have thought those people exist?

Mental Morph helps you problem-solve creatively, course-correct when things go wrong and navigate uncertainty without spiralling into panic. Some people thrive in unpredictable situations, instinctively adjusting, while others freeze in horror when plans get derailed. I mean, how dare someone change their mind about something we have been working on for almost a year? Of course, that has never happened a gazillion times during my career.

At its strongest, Mental Morph ensures resilience, adaptability and a solution-focused mindset. It allows people to pivot rather than resist, making challenges feel like exciting puzzles rather than catastrophic disasters. Without it? Well, let's just say life becomes a never-ending conveyor belt of disappointment and frustration. This superpower isn't just for naturally flexible thinkers. Anyone can strengthen cognitive adaptability, making change feel like an opportunity rather than a threat. Given how unpredictable the world is right now, this might be one to prioritise if this is a challenge for you.

The benefits of Mental Morph

When flexibility becomes a skill instead of a fluke, everything shifts, literally. Mental Morph isn't as simple as just going with the flow, it's about having the mindset of not falling apart the moment someone says, 'The deadline's moved.' People who master Mental Morph aren't imagining violent deaths for their colleagues who dare to change their minds, with such vivid detail it would make *Final Destination* look like a kid's film.

Instead of seeing uncertainty as chaos, this superpower reframes it as opportunity. Whether it's unexpected feedback, shifting plans, or a full-blown schedule derailment, Mental Morph keeps you adaptable, steady and solution-focused. Here's what happens when you develop the superpower of Mental Morph:

1. **Creative problem-solving becomes second nature:** You're not stuck trying to force old solutions to new problems. You know those people who say, 'We've always done it this way.' Yes, they are irritating. If that's you, sorry-not-sorry. Having Mental Morph means you come up with creative solutions quickly and easily pivot in response to feedback.
2. **You handle shifting priorities without losing momentum:** Plans will change, because that's life, and people are involved, who are unpredictable. Strong adaptability means you can change course without having to go back to the start. Ever heard of the corporate jargon of 'moving the goalposts'? Mental Morph superheroes are unfazed by this.
3. **Stress goes down, clarity goes up:** Rigid thinkers wrestle with uncertainty and end up exhausted by what they can't control. Mental

Morph removes the emotional resistance to change, helping you respond calmly to the unexpected without spiralling into frustration.

4. **Teamwork and collaboration become smoother:** It's easier to work with other people when you're not clinging to your way or the highway. Mental Morph helps you stay open to different viewpoints and bounce between ideas without taking it personally or digging in defensively. We've all met those people who refuse to change a decision because they don't want to lose face. With Mental Morph, you won't be one of those people.
5. **You become someone people count on during uncertainty:** In working environments, the most valuable people aren't the ones who always have a plan. It's the ones who can adapt when the plan goes sideways, which it often does. That's a prime example of a good leader, and it's the type of person people willingly follow.

Mental Morph isn't about pretending you love chaos. It's about being the person who can navigate it with purpose, calm, and clarity, with no meltdown required. Once mastered, adaptability becomes your edge.

The drawbacks of not developing Mental Morph

When adaptability is missing, life feels like a never-ending plot twist, and not the fun, binge-worthy kind.

Every change, however small, lands like a disruption instead of a detour. Instead of adjusting with ease, rigid thinking kicks in, causing friction, fatigue and the mental equivalent of shouting, 'I had a plan!' into the void. Without Mental Morph, even the simplest shift in direction can feel you've been asked to rebuild your entire routine from scratch. Here's what happens when Mental Morph is underdeveloped:

1. **You treat every change like an emergency:** Minor adjustments become massive roadblocks. Whether it's a delayed train, a surprise meeting or a last-minute change to dinner plans, the reaction is the same: panic, annoyance and an overwhelming urge to cancel everything. Ever had a manager like that? Oh. My. God. That's all I'll say on the matter, for ... libel reasons.
2. **Feedback feels like personal criticism:** When flexibility is limited, constructive feedback hits like a personal attack. Instead of using it to grow, you get stuck in a defensive loop that says, 'They just don't get how I work.' And then growth stalls. Same approach. Same mistakes. Same results. This is especially common for ADHDers who struggle with rejection sensitivity.
3. **You cling to broken strategies because they're familiar:** Even when a plan is clearly falling apart, rigid thinking doubles down. 'But this is how we've always done it' becomes the

hill to die on. The ability to easily pivot wanders off aimlessly into the forest, never to be seen again, leaving behind frustration and wasted energy in its place.

4. **Switching tasks feels like rebooting your entire brain:** Without strong Mental Morph, moving from one task to another feels like being unplugged and restarted. Transitioning becomes exhausting, slow, and mentally noisy. Projects get abandoned mid-way, because it's too difficult or you can't be bothered. 'That sofa looks too inviting right now' is a mantra I could live by some days – well, most days, but who's counting?
5. **Teamwork and your reputation takes a hit:** In group settings, inflexibility shows itself quickly. Struggling to adapt to new directions, different perspectives, or collaborative shifts makes working with others feel tense and unproductive. While others roll with it, rigid thinkers stall progress and quickly develop a reputation for being 'difficult to work with'. And nobody wants to be known as that, well perhaps sociopaths, but that's one for me to unpack with my therapist.

Without Mental Morph, life becomes a series of reactions instead of responses. You're not just resisting change, you're being dragged by it. But flexibility doesn't mean chaos. It means handling what's thrown at you with calm, clarity, and creativity.

And when you build that skill, chaos feels a lot more manageable.

ADHD and Mental Morph

For ADHD minds, cognitive flexibility isn't as simple as 'go with the flow', which for me will see the red mist descend if said in a patronising way. Us ADHDers all have those trigger terms, don't we?

Instead of seamlessly transitioning from one thing to the next, ADHD-working memory locks onto whatever is currently happening, making change feel like an unwanted interruption. Therefore, some people with ADHD can hyper-focus effortlessly on interesting tasks, yet struggle to move on to something less engaging.

Hyper-focus is one of ADHD's most powerful strengths, but it comes with a serious drawback: difficulty in shifting gears. Once locked onto a task, switching to something else feels like fighting against gravity. Even when the next responsibility is urgent, the brain doesn't want to let go of that juicy and exciting piece of work, which is fuelling your dopamine addiction. So, task-switching can cause frustration, delays and even total avoidance.

For neurotypical minds, shifting between responsibilities can feel natural, but for ADHD brains, it's like a mental reboot. The strain of disengaging from one focus and preparing for another isn't just irritating, it's draining. This is the reason I always feel tired and it has absolutely nothing to do with me being in my late forties.

For ADHD individuals, Mental Morph isn't about forcing task-switching to feel easier, it's about building flexibility techniques that make those transitions more manageable. Instead of getting stuck in cycles of frustration, developing the right strategies turns adaptability into something structured, predictable, and far less exhausting. And who doesn't want that? So, how do we beat our brains? We use the FLIP Circuit.

The FLIP Circuit

When plans unravel, deadlines shift or that 'quick update' turns into a full-blown strategy overhaul, your brain either panics or pivots. The FLIP Circuit gives your mind a proven route to follow when change lands on your desk uninvited. It transforms adaptability from a reactive scramble into a practised, repeatable flow. Because the real flex isn't pretending you love chaos, it's being able to handle it without spiralling. Don't worry, I'm not trying to turn you into one of those 'I love change' types, because we ADHDers will never be those people.

Here's how the circuit runs:

F = Feel the shift

Change arrives. Cue eye twitch. But before the overthinking starts or your brain screams 'NO!', this first step is about not fighting reality. Acknowledge that things are no longer going to plan in the safe space that is your head, as people can't read minds. Not yet, anyway. Sit with it for a few seconds and breathe.

1. **Don't waste your energy resisting the obvious:** Change is here, waving at you, demanding your attention. Think of it as the feisty auntie who asks really inappropriate questions about your love life. Yeah, do you have one of those as well?
2. **Give your brain a second to pause and reset:** Instead of diving into panic-mode. It's easy to do, but you don't need to run around the house screaming. Trust me, all you will get is a dirty look from your cat for disturbing her twelfth nap of the day.
3. **Reframe it in your mind:** This isn't disruption, it's an adjustment to progress. The world has not ended. Change is inevitable and is now part of daily life. Reframing it in your mind will help in how you process your response to it.

The faster you recognise the change without resistance, the easier the rest becomes.

L = Let it go

It's time to embrace your inner Elsa. There is a GIF of her twirling with the text 'let it go' which I send to colleagues when they get frustrated because someone has changed their mind about something. I send it a lot! There are leaders who change their minds constantly, and they are incredibly irritating, but do you really care? Like, deep down, do you care? If you won the lottery tomorrow, would you still be here? That's not to say you don't love your job. I love mine, but I win a million quid and I'll be waving goodbye. This is what you can do to channel that inner Elsa:

1. **Stop mentally replaying what should have worked:** It didn't. Lessons learned are great and all that, but you don't need them for everything. Ever done one of those exercises at the end of a project and wonder what happens to that document? If you know what happens, please tell me, because when the next project rolls around, I am not seeing any lesson learning in action.
2. **Reclaim that headspace:** Shift focus to 'What now?' It's important to look forward, rather than living in the good old days. I've seen this when companies go through rapid growth and people try to live in the past. We've seen humans evolve. So do companies.
3. **Drop the ego**: We all have one, no matter what you think. Some have one that is the size of a small solar system. Yeah, you know that guy as well, don't you? What I mean here is it's about changing approach, not giving up.

People will respect you more for admitting something isn't working.

I = Integrate the new

Change often comes with new data: feedback, evolving goals, and different perspectives. This phase is about absorbing new information without freaking out, sulking or slapping a sarcastic Post-it on your forehead that says 'Told you so'. (See, they have multiple purposes, although I do not recommend using them this way with your boss, or their boss for that matter.)

1. **Listen without assumption:** Let the new information land before reacting. I will often have a Post-it nearby which says, 'DO NOT SPEAK', as a visual prompt. This helps me take some thinking time, even if my initial reaction to what someone has said is pathological rage.
2. **Ditch the defensiveness:** This isn't about being wrong, it's about getting better. People respect openness and transparency, and if they don't, they are the problem.
3. **Adapt in real-time:** Quick course corrections save hours of unnecessary struggle. Take a moment to absorb, and then use that fast-thinking brain of yours to change approach.

P = Pivot with intention

Now the magic happens. You've acknowledged the shift. Let go of the broken plan. It's time to move with clarity. The pivot isn't frantic and emotion-driven, it's decisive and logical.

1. **Choose your next step with purpose, not panic:** Don't be driven by emotions. Listen to what your body is telling you. If your heart rate is still elevated, and you are imagining fire and brimstone, take a breather before deciding. You'll thank me later.
2. **Move into the next task:** Without your brain feeling like it's been thrown out of a moving vehicle. That's not fun. Well, I'm guessing. I did a few recklessly impulsive things in my youth, but that was not one of them.
3. **Build momentum:** Through small, logical decisions that say, 'Yes, I've got this.' Or whatever works for you. I'm not really one of those morning mirror affirmation people, but I have given myself a round of applause for my uber impressive change resilience skills – when there is nobody else around, of course.

Why the FLIP Circuit works

Most people fear change because they associate it with losing control. But the FLIP Circuit gives you back the control. Not by forcing things to stay the same, but by teaching you to respond with confidence when they don't.

When mastered, the FLIP Circuit turns chaos into choreography. Instead of bracing yourself for the next curveball, you think, 'Let's flip this.' Okay, nobody says that, but you get what I mean. I want these cheat codes to be memorable and FLIP has many connotations which can help with that.

Not ready for the FLIP Circuit?

Mental Morph isn't a natural skill. Some people effortlessly adjust when things change, while others feel attacked by sudden shifts in plans. If cognitive flexibility is a struggle, it doesn't mean you're doomed to panic every time life throws a curveball, it just means you need the right foundational skills before adaptability feels effortless. The personal effectiveness skills that will make Mental Morph second nature are: resilience, adaptability and self-coaching.

Resilience

Without resilience, every bump in the road feels like a personal insult from the universe. But resilience doesn't mean being immune to frustration; it's about getting back up without giving a TED Talk to your cat about how everything's ruined. Mental Morph relies heavily on the bounce-back factor. When you're flexible and resilient, you don't just survive the change; you use it to grow.

1. **You pivot fast instead of mourning what broke:** Resilient thinkers don't spend three hours mentally rewatching their failure like the latest Telenovela. *Jane the Virgin*, anyone? Loved that show. Add it to your watchlist. Trust me. The drama of that show is like what goes on inside your ADHD brain.
2. **You get unstuck before the spiral starts:** When frustration hits, resilience is the ability to breathe, reset and ask, 'Right, what's next?' rather than rage-texting your group chat about how your entire day has imploded, although that can feel therapeutic.
3. **You make forward progress faster:** You don't waste your mental battery sulking over version one of the plan; you jump straight into building the upgrade. Someone sent me version fifteen of something last month, asking for help, as they were 'going round the houses a bit'. I was ever so polite and professional, but if this book had already been published, I would have sent them a copy.

So, how do we build resilience? It takes time and effort, and there will be moments when you wonder if the skill has taken annual leave. It is something that can be very context specific in terms of its effectiveness. You need to keep working at it, so here are some pointers:

1. **Reframe failure as feedback:** What didn't work is often exactly what teaches you the most. It's not personal, just information. We make mistakes. It's part of life, but we need to learn from them. It shouldn't just be a time when a manager or partner points out what we did wrong, we need to take accountability even when someone isn't around to call us out.
2. **Build bounce-back speed in everyday situations:** Missed your train? Spilled coffee on your notes? Use those moments to practise the quick recovery reflex. Those things can be incredibly frustrating, although I can never understand when people get angry at missing a tube train. There is another coming in two minutes. It's those trivial little things which give us good practice for building bounce-back, so it's less challenging for something bigger.
3. **Recognise when your logic's been hijacked by frustration:** Pause. Reboot. Ask: what can I do next? Not: why does this always happen to me? The universe is not out to get you, but if you have the mindset that you are doomed, or, 'This day is a write-off', then you're more likely to manifest it becoming a reality.

Adaptability

Adaptability isn't about pretending to love chaos. It's about not letting it knock you flat on your back every time it shows up. When you've got it, you roll into new situations without freezing up. For Mental Morph to work, adaptability needs to be something you practise, not something you hope turns up on the day.

1. **You adjust quickly:** Somebody can drop a huge metaphorical bomb on you, and you can just roll with it without feeling blindsided or that the world has ended from said bomb. We've all had managers who seem to have a bag full of grenades and just toss them at will. People with the skill of adaptability aren't fazed by that.
2. **You don't hit mental roadblocks at every turn:** Shifting tasks, switching perspectives, or handling last-minute requests doesn't leave you plotting someone's demise. You can just get on with it. I envy you people so much. I can do it most days, but some days, not so much.
3. **You see options instead of obstacles:** While others freeze or moan, you spot the workaround. This commands respect from leaders who want to hear solutions, not problems.

Doesn't that all sound wonderful? But it is difficult to master, or we'd all be adaptability wizards. This is not a skill you can develop overnight, but here are some tips to get you started, so your brain stops arguing with reality and starts, hopefully, working with it:

1. **Deliberately push your own boundaries:** Try taking a different route to work, mix up your routine by going to the gym at a different time of day, or work somewhere new in the office for a change. This will help to train your brain to be more adaptive to change, yet you are still in control.
2. **Start saying 'yes' to change, even when it feels awkward:** Think of it as an improvisation. Ever had a day of just saying 'yes' to things? I did that once when I was travelling in Australia and had one of the best days of my life doing some very crazy things, such as diving into rapids and re-enacting the old Timotei adverts. If you know, you know.
3. **Practise micro-adaptability exercises:** That sounds a bit too technical, I know, but what I mean here is to try the 'little and often' approach to change. Change your routine subtly, and build things up. Practising our adaptability will put us in a stronger mindset for when the big changes come out of nowhere, because they will.

Self-coaching

Self-coaching is the quiet MVP behind every moment you don't completely lose the plot. It's not about chirpy self-help mantras or pretending everything's fine. It's about nudging your brain into gear on purpose. Mental Morph doesn't run on autopilot. It needs you in the driving seat. As someone who is an accredited coach, I have seen the value coaching can bring to someone, but self-coaching is something I now couldn't live without.

1. **You're in charge:** Don't wait to feel ready for change, and see what happens when it blindsides you. Change doesn't send you a calendar invite two weeks before it turns up. We ADHDers love to catastrophise, so this is the perfect opportunity to talk through all the crazy things which you think could happen.
2. **Reset the story:** Instead of getting stuck in the spiral of avoidance, self-coaching helps you step back and look at the situation objectively. It aids self-motivation. Talking things through, even to ourselves, can build our confidence in deciding.
3. **Flexibility feels structured:** You shift gears like you're in charge, not like someone who just woke up from deep sleep and doesn't know where they are. We talk something out, and we take out the emotional heat by expressing it, but not being driven by it.

You do not need a coaching qualification to develop this skill. Good managers should use coaching skills as standard. We are naturally inquisitive as humans and it's a lot easier to ask yourself questions than someone else, especially if there is nobody around to hear your answers. Here are some tips to develop your self-coaching skills:

1. **Create your own ritual:** A phrase, a deep breath, a movement. Something you do to signal to your brain that it's time to shift focus. Find what works for you. I like to walk around inside the house whilst I talk things out, or just think. It also gets my step count up, so double win.
2. **Reflect after each change:** Ask yourself if how you responded felt smooth or chaotic. Write down your thoughts and be curious about your response, not critical. This should be one of those times you write down your thoughts, intending to read it back.
3. **Set intentional prompts:** Before switching approach in response to the change, take a second to set a new goal. This will help your brain focus on the endgame and become less overwhelmed with trying to process your emotions.

With resilience, adaptability, and self-coaching in your ever-expanding toolkit, you've got sound foundations to apply the FLIP Circuit cheat code and become a true master of Mental Morph.

Action

In the next week, deliberately interrupt one of your own routines, expectations, or plans **on purpose**. I know, but trust me on this one. It doesn't have to be dramatic. The key is to catch yourself in that moment of change resistance and activate the FLIP Circuit right then and there. But this won't have any work-related consequences, so you can stumble and make mistakes. It's how we learn. This could be switching up your gym routine, going somewhere else for your morning coffee, doing the weekly food shop in-person instead of online. You choose, but make sure it's something that feels a bit uncomfortable, or the exercise won't work.

Here's how to run the circuit:

1. **Feel:** Notice the moment your brain starts to resist the change. Pause, breathe, and remind yourself: this is just a change, not a disaster.
2. **Let it go:** Feel free to sing that. I'm not here to judge. Acknowledge that what you thought was going to happen no longer is; or it is happening, but something is different. You can't go back. Let. It. Go.
3. **Integrate:** Look at what's actually happening instead of what was supposed to happen. Don't react, adjust.

4. **Pivot:** Move forward with the new supermarket, gym time, coffee shop or whatever you chose. And do it with a positive mindset. This is not the end of the world. At the end of the day, coffee is just coffee. Yes, I really did just say that.

After you've done this exercise, take some time to reflect. What threw you? What worked? Where did the resistance creep in? The more aware you are of your FLIP moments, the quicker this circuit becomes second nature. Are you going to revert, stick with the change or FLIP again?

What's next?

Are you ready to get into the last superpower? I've left the worst until last. Well, for me. This is the villain of my story, and continues to derail me every day, but of course I have one final cheat code. So, grab a drink of your choosing, sit back, relax and get ready for the superpower of Impulse Shield.

Chapter 11

The Power of Impulse Shield

As mentioned before, Impulse Shield is the ultimate battle before you save the prince from the tower, and I still haven't fully conquered it. Sometimes I can do it well, and then something, or usually someone, will throw me off my game. It's the superpower I see many fellow ADHDers struggle with.

Impulse Shield is the ability to pause before acting, regulate emotions effectively and make thoughtful choices rather than instinctive ones. It's being able to filter what we say before we say it. Now, wouldn't that superpower be an outstanding one to master?

Impulse control is the executive function that prevents impulse-driven disasters, ensuring that decisions are calculated instead of knee-jerk responses. Some people seem to naturally handle stress, frustration and distractions with an almost eerie level of composure. Watching them calmly process everything before responding is like witnessing a psychological masterclass in emotional control. For the rest of us? We blurt things out mid-conversation, impulse-buy pointless crap, and react first before fully assessing what's happening.

Impulse Shield isn't just about avoiding poor decisions, it's about strengthening self-awareness and control, making reactions deliberate rather than chaotic. Without it, life becomes a series of questionable choices, followed by internal regret and the desperate hope that nobody remembers what just happened; they always remember.

At its strongest, Impulse Shield ensures composure, discipline, and clarity in decision-making. It prevents emotional responses from dictating behaviour, reducing stress, frustration, and accidental self-sabotage. Instead of being controlled by impulse, people with this superpower control their own actions, making choices with awareness rather than reckless urgency. I have one question: who are these people?

Mastering this skill is an ongoing battle for me. Some superpowers in this book came naturally, others took work, but Impulse Shield? This one has required constant effort, strategy, and self-reflection. Because impulse control doesn't feel fun when you're someone who thrives on fast decisions and immediate action. But, at its core, Impulse Shield is about ensuring that fast decisions are smart ones, not just instinctive reactions that create unnecessary chaos. Just ask my husband what it's like living with someone whose filter is constantly on the blink. I did just ask him, and he responded with one word: exhausting.

The benefits of Impulse Shield

Impulse Shield is your personal pause button. The moment between urge and action where your future self either says, 'Thank you!' or screams internally. When this superpower is strong, you don't lose your cool in difficult conversations, you don't hit 'send' before rereading that spicy email and you don't accidentally commit to hosting an event when you meant to just express mild interest. Self-regulation doesn't kill spontaneity, it gives it boundaries. And in high-stakes moments, those boundaries are a godsend. Here is another list of five benefits, you know, because I had to.

1. **Improved decision-making under pressure:** Instead of acting on gut reactions and hoping for the best, Impulse Shield gives you space to think. That flash of annoyance? It passes. That sudden 'Yes!' to something you didn't want to do? Delayed. You gain the ability to pause, assess and make choices that align with logic, not just emotion. I have got better at asking for some time to reflect, and most people are agreeable to that. If they aren't? Recommend they read this chapter as well.
2. **Stronger relationships and smoother communication:** You no longer leave

conversations thinking, 'Why did I say that?' Emotional regulation gives you a filter without making you robotic. You respond thoughtfully, even when annoyed, and that makes you easier to work with, talk to, and be around. Someone once told me they were worried about telling me something because of how I might react. That was a wake-up call. I never want people to feel that way about me.

3. **Better focus and fewer distractions:** Impulse Shield is your internal bouncer, deciding who, or what, gets into the nightclub that is your brain. When a 'quick' scroll threatens to derail your day or an exciting idea tries to pull you away from something important, you can actually say no. Or at least ... later. We all know the best nights out are the ones which aren't planned, but we don't need to say yes every time someone asks.
4. **Increased follow through:** You stop abandoning tasks halfway through because something shinier came along. The ability to override urges helps you finish what you start and follow plans through with intention. You become that person who does the thing instead of just promising yourself you will get to it before an arbitrary date, but in reality, it has been on your list for a decade.
5. **Stronger credibility:** People notice when you're composed. When you regulate your impulses, you project calm, confidence, and

control, even if internally you're screaming and wishing you had the power of molecular combustion. Think of Piper in *Charmed*! That steadiness builds trust, especially in pressure-heavy environments where split-second reactions can make or break progress.

Mastering Impulse Shield gives you the tools to navigate life with more clarity, composure and consistency, but when that shield is weak or missing entirely, it's a different story. For every benefit it brings, there's a drawback waiting on the other side when self-regulation slips. And those drawbacks? They have a sneaky habit of turning minor moments into major episodes of drama.

The drawbacks of not mastering Impulse Shield

When your Impulse Shield is not fully developed, life becomes a highlight reel of 'I probably shouldn't have done that.' Yeah, we've all been there, haven't we?

You decide too quickly, say things you immediately regret, and wonder how one notification led to three hours of internet spiralling. Without regulation, your brain becomes a pinball machine: flashing, noisy, and unpredictable. Here's what happens when you're running without a shield:

1. **Snap decisions that lead to instant regret:** You speak before thinking. Commit before

checking the diary. React before processing. And then? You spend the next twenty-four hours playing the mental replay reel and drafting apology messages in your mind. I prefer to play out the dramatic scenario in my head where it's safe and then do the complete opposite.

2. **Conflict that didn't need to happen:** One snappy comment, one defensive reply, one slightly too-sarcastic joke and suddenly you're in a full-blown misunderstanding. Impulsivity in conversations doesn't just spark friction, it adds extra work as damage control. Here's an amusing anecdote. I once apologised to someone for snapping at them, and they replied, 'You're the politest anyone has been to me today.' I was like, WTF? And insisted they come for a drink after work so they could vent. They thanked me the next day.
3. **Lost time, focus, and money:** Distractions become decisions. You open your phone, just to check, and suddenly it's tomorrow. You buy the thing you don't need, abandon the task halfway through, and wonder why your to-do list feels like a personal attack. 'Is that Amazon again?' is a common sentence uttered in the Lennon-Barrett household, but we are both guilty of that one.
4. **Abandoned goals and half-finished plans:** Impulse-driven minds chase instant gratification, which is great for snacks, not so

much for long-term success. I'm not even sure it's great for snacks. I still haven't broken out of the supper tray habit I had as a kid. Except now it's not a tray. Just repeat visits to the kitchen, you know, to get my steps up.

5. **Workplace credibility takes a hit:** When you react before thinking, interrupt meetings with off-the-cuff comments, or change course without explanation, it chips away at trust. Colleagues don't just want talent, they want consistency. And impulsivity often sends the opposite signal. Being someone who delivers excellent work isn't enough if they don't know which version of you they are going to get each day.

Impulse Shield isn't about suppressing your emotions, it's having control over them. Although the drama can be fun sometimes, there are usually consequences and, if our intrusive thoughts are in charge of our behaviour, it can be quite damaging. Memory wiping and reversing time are not ADHD superpowers - well, not yet, anyway.

ADHD and Impulse Shield

For ADHD minds, impulse control isn't just tough, it's one of the hardest executive functions to control. Thoughts move faster than the ability to filter them, emotions process instantly, and actions often happen before there's time to consider the consequences. It's not about being reluctant to pause, it's about feeling like the brain won't let you.

One of the biggest struggles is the instant reaction reflex. ADHD makes it nearly impossible to slow down responses, meaning decisions happen before logic can catch up. Speaking before thinking, clicking on distractions without hesitation, or jumping into an impulsive action before fully assessing the situation. This is why ADHD individuals often struggle with impulse-driven mistakes. It's not because there's no awareness, it's because the brain rarely pauses before reacting. Some of my biggest regrets in life come from this. It was this uncontrollable emotional dysregulation which caused me to smash windows at home and subsequently get kicked out at sixteen.

Impulsivity also affects spending habits and time management. ADHD brains struggle with resisting immediate dopamine rewards, making impulsive purchases more frequent. If I buy one more piece of crap off Instagram which we don't need I am sure my husband will divorce me. It's not that priorities don't matter, it's that short-term gratification overrides logical reasoning, making distractions almost impossible to resist. I sometimes feel like most of these influencers get more than half their revenue from us ADHDers with no self-control.

Our brains are dopamine-driven, meaning distractions aren't just tempting, they feel necessary. The idea of waiting for a reward, focusing through boredom or delaying gratification is often intolerable, leading to impulsivity winning out every time. It's not that self-control doesn't exist, it's that resisting a tempting option requires significantly more mental effort than it does for neurotypical minds. And why should we wait? It's a question I ask myself every day.

Managing impulsivity requires intentional strategies, ensuring decisions are deliberate rather than reactive, and actions serve long-term goals rather than immediate urges. With the right strategies, impulse control stops being frustrating and starts becoming a powerful tool. And how can you develop those strategies? Let's look at our final cheat code.

Silent SCREAM

For every other superpower, I have used four components, such as DOPE and ECHO. Here, we are using six. And why are we doing that? Because there is no other word which better describes the cheat code you need for this superpower and this, at least for me, is the hardest to master. We need a bit more for this one.

Silent SCREAM gives you six distinct moments of mental control, each one designed to intercept the chaos before it takes over. It's quiet, deliberate, and effective. Here's how it works:

S = *Still*

The very first move is to do … nothing. No clicking 'Send'. No rolling your eyes. No adding-to-cart. Just freeze the action, even for a second. ADHD brains are wired for speed, so a split-second delay can feel like forever. But this step buys you time.

1. Physically pause. Don't act. Don't reply. Don't reach. Stillness disrupts the autopilot.
2. Use a sensory 'stop' cue. A hand gesture, a deep inhale, or literally say 'freeze' in your head. If I know I am having a difficult meeting, I will have 'STOP' written and visible in some way.

This is your interrupt signal. It doesn't have to be graceful, it just has to work.

C = Check

Now get curious. Every impulse has a trigger, usually emotional, sometimes chemical, occasionally just pure chaos. The goal here isn't to judge it but to notice what's fuelling it.

1. Ask yourself: What am I feeling right now? Not what you're doing, but what you're feeling. Don't start solutionising, which we love to do, just feel.
2. Common culprits? Frustration, panic, anxiety, FOMO, boredom, overstimulation, or sometimes ... just plain dopamine withdrawal.
3. Label it aloud if possible: 'This is stress.' 'This is overstimulation.' Naming it gives you control.

This tiny check-in gives shape to something previously invisible, making the impulse easier to handle.

R = Reframe

Now that you've named the urge, it's time to flip it. What's really happening here? Most of the time, the impulse isn't about what you're doing, it's about what you're avoiding, suppressing, or trying to resolve quickly. So let's redirect it with intention.

1. Want to fire off a blunt email? Draft it. Don't send it. Sleep on it. Future-you will be grateful. I've read some of these back and thought 'Thank f... I didn't send that.'
2. About to drop a shedload of cash on something random? Picture future-you looking at the receipt, asking, 'Why?' Or your significant other with that WTF scowl you just love them for.

You're not burying the reaction. You're reframing it into something smarter.

E = Evaluate

This is where logic joins the party. It took its time, and we know that, which is why we have all the steps before we get here. Look at the urge from a bird's-eye view. Not, 'Is this fun?' but 'Does this serve me?' You're allowed to want the thing, but you're also allowed to decide it's not worth it.

1. What are the consequences? Five minutes from now, five days from now, or five weeks? Are you looking at a happy dance or will you want to die of embarrassment and hibernate in a cave?
2. Who else does this affect? Are you going to clean up an emotional, social or financial mess afterwards? Our ADHD brains can be very dramatic when thinking of consequences, so use this to your advantage.

Evaluation isn't about guilt, it's about perspective, and sometimes we need that inside voice saying, 'Really?'

A = Adjust

Now that you've stepped back, make an adjustment. I know, I know, but sometimes these cheat codes just write themselves! This adjustment doesn't mean overhauling your life, it means a tiny redirect. Think of it like reversing out of a cul-de-sac, rather than keeping going and ending up destroying someone's living room.

1. Swap the impulse for a reward-delaying action: 'Save to basket' instead of 'Buy'. I would say use 'Wishlist' but if you are like me, you completely forget that thing is there, and discover you wanted to buy a colour printer four years ago.
2. Use the urge productively, channel it into something you'll enjoy doing. This will fuel

your dopamine and helps to get any built-up emotions out in a healthy way.

This is the power move. It's the moment you take back control. It's an amazing feeling when you master it. I don't claim to do it every time, but it feels good when you do it. I would even say it's better than chocolate, but keep that to yourself.

M = Move

The last step is to take action, but make it a considered one. You don't need to over-explain. You don't need to be perfect. You just need to move forward on purpose. Movement completes the cycle and tells your brain: I'm in charge of my emotions now.

1. Choose an intentional action, even if it's just walking away. This can be very empowering. I've done it, even when I wanted to blow things up. I feel better for the decision I made.
2. Use movement to reset: a stretch, a walk, a simple change of scenery. This isn't about distracting yourself, but focusing on moving your body instead of your spiralling thoughts helps a lot.

The goal is never perfection. It's regulation. And regulation means progress, without the hangover of regret.

Why Silent SCREAM works

Because it's simple enough to remember under pressure, and powerful enough to interrupt even the strongest impulses. You're not suppressing emotions, you're channelling them. I have used the word 'suppress' a lot when referring to impulse control, and that's deliberate.

Having spent many years not understanding why I felt such powerful emotions, and being told to 'Keep it to yourself', or the favourite, 'Boys don't cry', I know firsthand how unhealthy that is. You should never suppress your emotions. It's important to feel them. How you show those emotions to others is what we are focused on here.

Not ready for Silent SCREAM?

Impulse control doesn't just appear overnight. Sometimes, trying to self-regulate in the heat of the moment feels like putting out a fire with a thimble of water. And while Silent SCREAM is a solid strategy, it lands a lot better when you've got the right foundations under it.

That's where these three personal effectiveness skills come in. They act like support beams for your Impulse Shield. Skills that catch you before you spiral, help you process what's going on, and give you tools to steer yourself back on course. If jumping straight into Silent SCREAM feels like a leap too far, start here with assertiveness, mindfulness, and conflict resolution.

Assertiveness

Assertiveness happens when you finally stop bottling everything up until it explodes in an email you immediately regret. It's not about volume, power, or sounding like a TED Talk, it's about saying what you mean clearly, calmly, and confidently, before your emotions stage a hostile takeover. For ADHD minds, it can feel tricky: we either say too much too fast, or nothing at all until it bursts out sideways. Assertiveness gives that emotion a valid outlet, without creating drama.

1. **You speak with clarity, not confusion:** You say what you feel, rather than acting out what you're struggling to articulate. This is about being articulate with making your point, so the words you choose are conscious, and not coming out before you've thought about them.
2. **You reduce the risk of emotional leakage:** There's not another word which works there, so snigger away. This is about reducing the likelihood of no boiling-point breakdowns over something as minor as not doing the dishes.
3. **You build credibility and self-respect:** The more you practise expressing yourself directly, the less you second-guess every conversation afterwards. You can walk away

feeling positive about your behaviour in that moment, even if the other person was dysregulated.

Assertiveness remains one of those training courses which, like time management, is always full, but the audience is different. With time management, you will get people at all levels of the organisation attending. For assertiveness, it's mostly people earlier in their career. There's an unspoken expectation that people in management or senior roles should be expected to do this without question, but it's a tricky skill to develop. Here are some tips for developing your assertiveness:

1. **Use 'I' statements to stay grounded:** Instead of 'You're ignoring me', try, 'I feel overlooked in this conversation.' It's clearer, softer, and much harder to argue with. One thing I get across in training is that you can't question someone's intent, as you don't know what's going on inside their head, just like they don't know what's going on in yours. Probably a good thing. If you reframe with how their behaviour affects you, you're less likely to get a defensive response.
2. **Set boundaries without the guilt narrative:** 'I can't take that on right now' is assertiveness. 'Maybe, if nobody else can do it and you're really desperate ...' is a panic response. You don't have to people-please all

the time. That's a very British thing. I've always been fascinated by the way people from different countries and cultures say no, and having worked for global companies, I know it's important to prepare for those differences.

3. **Watch tone and pace:** ADHDers speak fast. Slowing down your delivery makes you sound more considered and gives you time to think as you go. This will help you sound more credible, as it will take the emotion out of your vocal pitch without sounding like a corporate robot. Nobody wants to come across like that.

Assertiveness isn't about being right, it's about being clear. It keeps your voice steady when your mind's racing and your pulse is sprinting. And the best part? When you use it with confidence, people listen differently, too.

Mindfulness

Mindfulness isn't about sitting cross-legged on a yoga mat, breathing in a field of lavender. It's about awareness. Being fully present and clocking what your brain is doing before your behaviour joins the party. When you're mindful, you notice the emotion before the email is sent, the tension before the sarcastic reply lands, and the trigger before the impulse takes over. This is something I struggle with. I once did a 'Day in the Life of ADHD' exercise and told everyone we were going to meditate. They gave me 'the look' before getting into position. I then blasted heavy metal music to show that's what my brain is like all the time. The response was hilarious. I've got better at it now, and although I can't meditate for long durations I can use mindfulness techniques to take a pause before I embrace my inner Taurus and run at the problem like a bull in a china shop.

For impulse control, this skill is gold. It shifts your brain out of autopilot and into observation mode. Essential for anyone who acts first and processes later.

1. **You respond instead of react:** There's just enough space between 'feel it' and 'do it' for clarity to squeeze in. It can just take a few seconds of you asking yourself, 'Is this really a good idea?' From personal experience, the answer is usually: NO.
2. **You notice your triggers earlier:** Instead of wondering why you keep saying yes or snapping in meetings, you see it happening in real time. I find taking notes or doodling helps here, because it allows the brain a few seconds to calm down.
3. **You stop fighting thoughts and start managing them:** Mindfulness doesn't mean having no impulses. It means being aware of them without letting them take control.

This is one of those skills that I will often get an eye roll about and, to be honest, that was once me as well. But I have experienced and seen the value this brings to managing your emotions and impulses. It's also valuable out of work as well, when you feel like someone is trying to goad you to snap. With mindfulness skills, someone in that interaction is going to be disappointed in themselves, and it won't be you. Here are some tips for developing mindfulness.

1. **Practise micro-awareness daily:** Pause for 15 seconds before you click, speak, or swipe. Ask, 'What am I feeling?' and, 'What am I about to do?' That two-question check-in is powerful.
2. **Name your top five impulse triggers:** Boredom? Rejection? Deadlines? All the above? Once you know them, they're no longer invisible tripwires.
3. **Use existing habits:** Link mindfulness to something you already do, like brushing your teeth or making coffee. Take ten seconds during that habit to just observe, with no need to solve anything.

Mindfulness doesn't eliminate our impulsive tendencies, but it makes them easier to spot, slow down, and think before acting. Put your pessimistic hat to one side and give this one a go.

Conflict resolution

Some of us would rather chew tinfoil than engage in difficult conversations. For ADHD brains especially, conflict can trigger impulsive communication: defensive replies, dramatic exits or apologising for things we didn't actually do. That's why conflict resolution isn't just helpful, it's a self-regulation essential.

1. **You can stay composed when others get reactive:** Their escalation doesn't have to be yours. That's genuine power. We naturally mirror other people's behaviour, so if you stay calm and logical, there is a strong possibility it will calm the other person down. Not always. It can have the opposite effect, but you can't control other people's emotions, only your own.
2. **You're more likely to say what you mean instead of what's easiest:** Less people-pleasing, more authenticity. If we are in that logical, adult brain space, and not being driven by our emotions, we can get across our point whilst still being empathetic to the other person.
3. **You avoid impulse-laced conflict spirals:** The ones where you say too much, too fast, then replay it for the rest of time. I still cringe at a conversation I had twenty-seven years ago. Why does working memory have to

remember that, but not something I agreed to do five minutes ago?

How do you build this skill without becoming a full-time HR specialist? I've been one, and it's still difficult. It's not just neurodivergent brains which struggle with conflict. This is one which is a challenge for most people. Here's how to strengthen this skill through practical application:

1. **Learn to validate before disagreeing:** Try, 'I get where you're coming from, and here's my take ...' It disarms defensiveness instantly. Or, 'I know you feel upset by this. Let's talk it through.' This approach acknowledges a person's feelings, but doesn't admit responsibility for anything.
2. **Practise conflict drills with friends or a mentor:** Use past situations and ask, 'How could I have responded differently?' Low-stakes reflection builds high-stakes readiness. Put yourself in the other person's shoes and think about how it would feel to be on the receiving end.
3. **Watch your exit strategy:** Don't ghost, over-apologise, or go nuclear. Sometimes just saying, 'I need a few minutes to think' is enough to hold the boundary without shutting it down. This one has saved me many times. I can feel the pathological rage wanting to take complete control, but by just asking for a

time out, it gives me time to regulate my emotions.

Strong conflict resolution means your impulses don't hijack conversations anymore. You handle pressure like the calm one in the room, even if inside your head you still want to go on a murderous rampage. But nobody needs to know that, do they?

Action

Over the next week, identify one moment where you feel the pull of an impulse. That might be the urge to fire off an inflammatory email, say yes to something you don't actually want to do, reach for a random online purchase, or derail your plans for something shinier and dopamine-soaked.

When it hits, run the Silent SCREAM sequence:

1. **Still:** Freeze the instinct. Interrupt the pattern.
2. **Check:** Identify the emotion behind it. Name it out loud.
3. **Reframe:** Ask yourself what this impulse is really trying to fix or avoid.
4. **Evaluate:** Think long-term: Is this action helping or hurting you?
5. **Adjust:** Redirect the energy into a smarter alternative.
6. **Move:** Take a decision forward with intention, not urgency.

Then take two minutes after to reflect. What worked? What didn't? Where did your brain want to skip steps? That reflection is where the learning happens. Some parts of Silent SCREAM will be harder than others, so it's good to identify what you need to focus on developing. That self-awareness is half the battle won.

What's next?

Why have one superpower when you can have two? As I said earlier, this is not about having ultimate power, because we've all seen that doesn't end well for villain or hero. The ADHD superpowers complement each other, so you don't need to utilise them in isolation. In the next chapter, we'll explore how you pair the powers together to achieve even more brilliance.

Chapter 12

The Power Pairing

If I was one of the Mr Men, I would be Mr Greedy. I love my chocolate. It is the only thing I have never been able to give up for Lent, and I once did bread! I admire people who have the restraint to only have one square, but also question their life choices. How do they do it? I'm all in once that wrapper opens. So, with superpowers, one would never be enough for me. However, I'm also old enough to know better than being too greedy. Flashback to one-pound-a-drink nights at university. Remember those?

For that reason, I just changed the title of this chapter from 'The Power Stack' to 'The Power Pairing', which keeps things simple, yet impactful.

What is power pairing?

Power pairing is the intentional 'pairing' of two ADHD superpowers – yes, I know, I did it again, and probably not the last time in this book!

The aim of the pairing is that the superpowers complement each other and solve more than one executive function challenge at a time.

These pairings can come in different forms:

- A dominant strength and a development area.
- Two developing skills you're building in tandem.
- A pair which instinctively go together, such as planning and time management.

You don't need to master both at once. The magic comes from how they work together, supporting your brain's focus in ways a single superpower can't always achieve. It's important to remember everything we have covered so far. You can exceed expectations with a single superpower. But why only exceed expectations when you could be outstanding?

ADHD brains aren't built for isolation. What works best for us, are habits that reinforce each other, tools that talk to each other and strengths that plug each other's gaps. Otherwise it all feels like too much so we don't bother. So, when you combine two superpowers *intentionally*, you can achieve greatness.

The power pairings

You can be strong in one superpower and still be figuring out the other, or you might find both need work. You don't have to be a superpower master to get the benefits of power pairing. It's about using the combination which best suits you and your brain. It's not as simple as a fifty-fifty split, because that would be far too easy, wouldn't it?

Of course, I have given each pair their own name, because, well, it's me and I enjoy naming things.

The Planning Pair (Vision Crafter and Time Warp): for those who can see the future in vivid detail but can't get their diary to cooperate. This pair turns ideas into timelines, and strategy into action. Think of that uber efficient person, and this is probably what they are doing, even if unconsciously.

The Adaptive Pair (Mental Morph and Impulse Shield): for brains that thrive in an ever-changing world, but struggle with reactivity. This combination gives you the ability to pivot with intention but respond with clarity rather than regret. We've all been there, and you can't take it back once you've said it. Oh, how I wish I could!

The Tactical Pair (Focus Beam and Mind Vault): for deep thinkers who hyper-focus hard, but can forget what they're focusing on. This is about being able to get stuff done, but not lose sight of why we're doing it in the first place, and avoid those inevitable rabbit holes we ADHDers love.

Each pair solves a distinct problem. Yours might not be obvious at first, but once you find the pair that fits, you can turbocharge your strengths.

The Planning Pair

Vision Crafter and Time Warp are the planning dream team and, for an ADHD brain, they're pure catnip, or chocolate, if you're like me. One is about vision: seeing the big picture, spotting the ideal outcome and imagining how things could be. The other is about bending time to make progress, structuring chaos and giving that vision what it needs to succeed – time. On their own, each superpower is excellent, but when used together they are like rocket fuel.

Without structure to our ideas, the vision becomes fantasy. Without vision, structure becomes routine. Together, they fuel each other. You can map out a long-term goal and then slice it into manageable steps that actually fit into your day. Think of it like a staircase. You don't just jump to the top step, do you? And if you run up them, you could hurt yourself. I definitely don't do that all the time, and stumble at least once a week, usually carrying a glass of milk.

ADHD brains love a good plan; we just hate writing it. So we trick the brain by combining storytelling with scheduling. Deadlines become check-ins. And suddenly the stuff that used to feel boring now feels like we're building something exciting.

But it's not all simple and wonderful, or everyone would do it. The danger with this pairing is getting lost in the planning spiral. Editing the vision for perfection, overcomplicating the timeline, or colour-coding until you forget the goal entirely. A good indicator to me that one or more of my executive functions aren't working to their best ability is when I rewrite lists repeatedly, just making minor changes each time. It's a typical indicator that I am stressed, but by knowing this, it signals for me to stop and think about what's currently going on. Do I need a simple breather to re-prioritise a few things, or do I need to ask for help? What are your triggers that something isn't right? Give it some thought. It's important you know what they are.

The Adaptive Pair

Mental Morph and Impulse Shield make up the adaptive pairing built for brains that run at a million miles an hour, but need a filter to keep that momentum from spiralling into chaos. My filter needs to go into the repair shop most weeks. Thankfully, it's usually on the weekends when I have space from the sometimes-insufferable politics of the corporate world. I can reset, ready for the next week.

As I always say when I deliver emotional intelligence training, my impulse control score will always be low. I feel constantly irritated, but people don't need to know I feel that way. It's not about changing who you are as a person, but how you react to situations when they arise.

When requirements change mid-task, when a meeting goes off-course, when a deadline flips without warning, Mental Morph steps in with flexibility. It's the power that lets you pivot without panic. Impulse

Shield is the gatekeeper. It's what stops the reactive part of your brain from hijacking the moment with a comment, a decision or an emotional spiral that you'll regret five minutes later. To be fair, I'm surprised I still have a tongue with the amount of times I have to bite it each week.

For ADHD brains, this combination is deeply satisfying. You get the dopamine rush of change plus the emotional grounding of restraint. You still get to adapt, redirect, and improvise, but with control. I was supporting some colleagues with this recently. They were upset by someone's behaviour and, although I wanted to charge into battle for them, I knew it wouldn't change the outcome. Instead, we focused on how they could adapt to the change logically, but in a way which still keeps them on track for achieving their personal goals. It's not about the moral dilemma of giving in to someone's poor behaviour, but sometimes you have to be selfish and put your own wellbeing first.

The Tactical Pair

Focus Beam locks you into deep work with intensity, clarity and the tunnel vision that produces magic. Mind Vault becomes your back-up system, holding onto key details, tasks and threads that otherwise are sucked into the vortex, never to be seen again.

Focus Beam gives you the gift of depth but, without Mind Vault, you risk forgetting why you dived so deep. The email that triggered the idea? Gone. The task that sparked the creative sprint? Lost in the ether. Mind Vault catches those threads before they unravel.

I'm not a massive planner with writing fiction, as I like the characters to take me where they want to go, but I've had experiences when I've been thirty thousand words in to a novel and realised it's not working. By having some prompts, such as 'In chapter three, these five things will happen', it gives me the flex to let the characters forge their own path. However, the outline gives me a mental checklist to ensure I miss nothing essential to the story, or that a character hasn't changed hair colour five times.

ADHD brains love this pairing because it mirrors their natural flow: intense bursts of attention followed by, 'Wait, what was I doing again?' There's dopamine from focus, and safety from memory. It's the rare combination that feels fast and supported.

To stay on track, treat Mind Vault like a companion to your focus time. Start each hyper-focus session with a summary of your goal. End each session with a review, not for perfection, but for retrieval. What changed? What did you promise? What's next? Adjust the plan if you need to, but build in that reflection time.

Other potential pairings

The power pairings covered here play to each other's strengths, reducing friction and amplifying follow through. But that doesn't mean you're limited to these three combinations.

One of the best things about working with these six superpowers is the ability to design your own pairings. You might not need adaptive flexibility right now. Maybe memory support and strategic planning are the real problem. So try different things. Mix. Match. See what clicks.

Here are a couple of additional pairings to get you thinking, but this is not an exhaustive list:

Time Warp and Focus Beam: For those of you who hyper-focus, but lose track of time. Focus Beam gives you the power of getting stuff done, but Time Warp adds the guardrails, helping prevent black hole productivity spirals and missed deadlines.

Mental Morph and Mind Vault: For the agile thinker whose ideas change every five minutes. Nick hides in the corner! Mental Morph gives you the flexibility to pivot, but Mind Vault ensures you capture the changes, so they don't vanish mid-thought and great ideas aren't lost forever.

There's no perfect combination, as we're all as different as our brains. Try a pairing. See how they play together. Keep what works. Scrap what doesn't. Your ADHD doesn't need a rigid framework, it needs a creative one. And pairing two powers is the fastest way to stop firefighting and start building something brilliant.

Action

Now that you've met the three core power pairs, it's time to see how they work in your world. We're not aiming for perfection, we're aiming for insight. So take the theory, pick a pairing, and put it to the test.

Over the next week, choose one real situation you are dealing with. Before you get started, take five minutes to get yourself in the right headspace and choose a power pairing. You don't need to do all three, even if you really, really want to!

1. **Vision Crafter and Time Warp:** Write your end goal, then break it into three realistic time-bound actions. Only that. Stick to what fits your actual schedule, not the fantasy version which says there are seventy-two hours in a day.
2. **Mental Morph and Impulse Shield:** Think about what could change. Don't just focus on the negatives, even if that is your general view of change. What will you do if things change? How will you pause before responding? Choose a visual cue to prompt you to pause mid-chaos.
3. **Focus Beam and Mind Vault:** Make your intention clear. What do you want to get out of this hyper-focus session? Choose one key outcome. The dopamine will be high and you'll want to commit to ten things, but just choose one. Create a space to log thoughts

as you go. This could be Post-its, voice notes, or a digital ideas board.

After you have completed the action, reflect. What worked? What didn't? Did the powers show up together, or did one overpower the other? There's no failure, just data. Nobody gets it right the first time and, even when you've perfected something, you can have an off day. We're human, and we make mistakes, but every misstep is an opportunity to learn and grow. Always remember that when you're trying these things out. We are quick to be self-critical, so this will be a challenge. You can always start with something small and build up. These superpowers are like muscles, you need to exercise them regularly.

What's next?

Probably an obvious one, but if you can pair powers, can you pair the cheat codes? Of course you can. Let me show you how that works.

Chapter 13

The Cheat Code Combos

If the ADHD superpowers shape how your brain thinks, then cheat codes are the magic ingredient which enables us to operate at maximum efficiency. They're the flexible tactics, the shortcuts, the rituals, and mindset tweaks that help ADHD brains stay upright in a world built for linear thinkers, which we most definitely are not. And why did I call them cheat codes? Because ADHD brains need the quickest way to get that fix of dopamine.

What these combined cheat codes will do for you is give you even more powerful tools to achieve your goals, or just simply get through the day, because that in itself can be challenging enough.

Colour Compass

The name of this one was obvious. For the others I have had to be more creative, but we'll get to that.

This mega cheat code blends Element Compass and Colour Codex together.

It creates a visual delivery strategy that matches how your ADHD brain processes information and handles tasks. One system gives you direction, the other gives you clarity.

For this combined cheat code, think of the colours representing different task types, and your element represents your default thinking style.

Wind

Creative, fast-thinking, and momentum-driven. Wind is brilliant at starting, but struggles with follow-through. These people are the gold medal champions of procrastination.

- **Pink (Priority):** Wind gets distracted by new ideas. Pink pulls focus back to what matters now. Keep those Post-its front and centre, so they are a constant visual reminder.
- **Orange (Order):** Wind brains hate linear planning, so orange creates a visual 'Do this first' path. If the consequences are clear, it helps the brain focus on the right order to get things done.
- **Green (Go):** Wind loves movement, so green fuels action. It's essential to use it intentionally, and not in a scattergun way.
- **Blue (Buffer):** Wind often abandons half-finished tasks, blue keeps them visible

without pressure. Don't keep them too visible or they'll distract you from the pink priorities.

Fire

Driven, bold, outcome-focused. Fire wants speed and impact, but can miss nuance and reflection. Think of someone who is followed by a robotic hoover cleaning up the debris they leave in their wake.

- **Pink (Priority):** Fire thrives here. Use it to channel ambitious productivity. But watch for burnout. Fire can be unstoppable once it gets going and sleep is important.
- **Orange (Order):** This colour helps Fire pace itself. Not everything is a sprint. Orange slows things down for better results. By breaking things down, you allow for reflection time before moving on to the next task.
- **Green (Go):** Fire needs this to maintain steady progress once the adrenaline dips. They can have dopamine crashes, and attention will quickly drift to something shiny. The green keeps things visible and acts as a motivator.
- **Blue (Buffer):** A Fire brain rarely waits, but it needs to. Use blue to park ideas and wait for input before acting. Sometimes, they need to be put out of sight, but not too far, so they don't become out of mind as well.

Rain

Structured, steady, plan-led. Rain people thrive on routine and clarity, but stall quickly when faced with chaos or vague expectations. They aren't mind readers and need to know what they are doing.

- **Pink (Priority):** Rain doesn't love firefighting, but they need to see what's urgent so they can prep ahead. Pink helps them focus on what must be done and avoids last-minute stress.
- **Orange (Order):** This is Rain's comfort zone. They're wired for sequencing, and orange Post-its let them organise tasks step-by-step. Perfect for working in clean, focused sprints. If only that was how every day was structured.
- **Green (Go):** Rain uses green to keep the core tasks flowing. They don't need novelty; they need visible progress. Green becomes the fuel for their day-to-day momentum.
- **Blue (Buffer):** Rain benefits from knowing what's parked. Because they stick to what's planned, Blue keeps pending tasks from being forgotten without overwhelming them. Using a 'car park' whiteboard works well, if you have the space, or use a digital solution.

Earth

Structured and detail-focused. Earth builds foundations, but can resist change or get stuck in planning loops. This is the person who walks around with seven different notebooks.

- **Pink (Priority):** Earth can over-plan without acting. Pink pushes execution and moves it to the front of the queue. Don't get caught in a planning spiral. One to-do list is enough, as is one notebook!
- **Orange (Order):** This is Earth's utopia. Sequence everything. Just be mindful not to over-complicate things. A restriction on the number of Post-its used will help keep focus.
- **Green (Go):** Keeps work progressing between milestones. Use green to avoid perfection-doom-spiralling. Not everything can be gold-plated. As I said before, perfection does not exist.
- **Blue (Buffer):** Earth rarely forgets completely, but things can get buried and can be remembered at an inopportune moment which derails focus time. Blue keeps lower-priority tasks visible, with less concerns of them being a distraction like they can be with the other elements.

Colour Compass isn't just a colour system, it's a personalised guide. The colours give context to your tasks. The elements give insight into your responses. When used together, they form a brain-friendly productivity model where you can get stuff done.

Memory Engine

This is the sweet spot between productivity and recall. The Memory Engine blends the hyper-focus benefits of DOPE with the retention power of ECHO, giving your brain the optimal conditions to start, sustain, and remember.

As you will see, trying to combine the DOPE Engine and the ECHO Index into a single name didn't quite work, but Memory Engine is a perfect name if I do say so myself. Here's how it works in practice.

You start by firing up your DOPE Engine:

- **Eliminate distractions:** Phone, background noise, or your partner asking if you've put the bins out, or replenished the drinks in the fridge.
- **Get organised:** Clean workspace, tools lined up and coffee in hand - or tea, if you're from the north of England.
- **Set your preference:** Comfy corner, Heart 90s radio station blasting and air conditioner on turbo. That is a purchase I do not regret making, even if in the UK you only need it for two weeks of the year.
- **Identify your endgame:** A cupcake, a few chapters from your latest book, an episode of your latest binge or just collapsing on the sofa knowing you achieved your goal.

Now you have the DOPE in full flow. Yes, you knew that was coming! Now is the time to apply the ECHO Index to keep yourself on track, and don't let your hyper-focus send you ten miles off course.

- **Emotional connection:** This could be the happiness of completing the task, the fear of not doing so if there are consequences or the humorous cat videos which you will watch when you're done.
- **Chunk the information:** It's easy to hyper-focus and do nothing else, but you need to be sensible to avoid burnout. For example, if I wanted to write five thousand words in a day, I could break this into one-thousand-word chunks, so I can have a mental checkpoint as I hit each milestone.
- **Hear it:** Talk through your plan aloud. By hearing it, you'll process its feasibility differently. Will it be successful? Are you setting yourself up for success or failure? You don't want to make things too easy, but we ADHDers are our own worst critic and nobody needs to hear from that judgy inside voice.
- **Organise it:** This is identical to the 'O' in DOPE. Make sure you have an environment in which you can thrive. This doesn't need to be a Norwegian forest, unless that's your thing, but it should be somewhere with limited distractions.

Look at the combination like this: DOPE gets you going, and ECHO makes sure it lasts. You don't want to be powering through tasks, hoping you remember everything which needs doing. Memory Engine turns fleeting focus into lasting impact. And the best part? You don't need spreadsheets or complicated software. You just need to build the right conditions so you can thrive.

Chaos Controller

This isn't just adaptability: it's regulated adaptability. I don't know why that made me think of the M&S adverts, but now you're thinking of them as well if you live in the UK.

The combination of FLIP Circuit and Silent SCREAM turns reactive spirals into responsive strategy, guiding your brain through unexpected change without burning the world down when you have that inevitable hissy fit. And, yes, I do include myself in this.

Chaos Controller is the power pairing which has helped me out of some tricky situations. As I have said before, I love change if I am driving it forward, but if it's being forced on me, and by people who have the emotional intelligence of a dial tone, I need this mega cheat code to stop me exploding.

You start with FLIP Circuit, because chaos usually arrives uninvited, so it's a change you need to adapt to. A meeting goes sideways. A decision gets reversed. A manager speaks to you like you're five years old. Let's not go there! Instead of spiralling into a dysregulated meltdown, FLIP gives you the system you need to consider the change. Here's a reminder:

- **Feel the shift:** Train your brain to acknowledge the change, but don't openly panic about it. This is about feeling, not reacting.
- **Let it go:** Process your emotions about the change, but don't linger on something which you can't control. Remember that it's a basic human reaction to resist change and not unique to ADHD brains.
- **Integrate the new:** Consider the change logically. How will this affect you and what do you need to do to integrate it into your world? It's happening, and you can't control that, but your reaction is something you have power over.
- **Pivot with intention:** Move forward, which could be telling yourself, 'I've got this,' getting excited about the challenge of the change, or simply accepting that you need to move forward and not give it any more headspace, which would be, 'I need to just get on with this.' You could also add, 'And I'll watch with glee when it all crashes and burns.' Which is okay if you say that in your head. Managers tend to get twitchy if you say that out loud.

Sounds too easy doesn't it? But the world doesn't work that way. A reaction brews. The change triggers something. A snarky comment bubbles up. That urgent email becomes a passive-aggressive manifesto, or someone asks, 'Are you okay?' in the most condescending way ever, and you wonder if it would be worth doing twenty years in prison. Not that I'm talking from experience here of course. This is where Silent SCREAM enters the chat.

Silent SCREAM wraps around the FLIP Switch to contain the impulse. This is how it works:

- **Still:** Interrupt the autopilot. Freeze the motion before the email's sent, the comment is made on the Teams call or the online checkout gets blessed with your money. Stillness stops things spiralling. I have shouted, 'Freeze!' before, not knowing I wasn't on mute. Yeah, that wasn't awkward.
- **Check:** Name what you're feeling, not just what you're doing. Stress? Ego? Boredom? Identifying the emotional trigger gives you power over it.
- **Reframe:** Flip the narrative. You're not being undermined, you're being asked to change something. Nobody is out to get you. That email doesn't need an angry retort, it needs a draft folder because we still need to get that rant out at some point.

- **Evaluate:** Think big picture. Yes, I used corporate jargon, but it works here. Ask yourself if this action will serve you five minutes from now, or leave you cleaning up a mess five days later? Regret is like a high-interest loan and I'm sure we all still cringe about something we did twenty years ago.
- **Adjust:** It doesn't need to be a dramatic switch, but hold the sarcasm! Turn impulse into intentionality without sacrificing your authenticity. You can still be yourself without hitting the big red button.
- **Move:** Take considered action, not reactive revenge. Whether it's breathing, switching tasks, or closing the Amazon app. Movement resets the impulse cycle. They are probably not thinking about you when they go home, so why give them headspace? I know it isn't easy, but plotting the downfall of today's mortal enemy doesn't serve you in the long run.

Chaos Controller doesn't shut down who you are, it keeps you from becoming the dramatic version of yourself your enemies would love to screenshot. I'm so happy I grew up in the last century, so most of my embarrassing moments were never immortalised on film, but we don't have that luxury any more. Always have that at the back of your mind. Nobody wants to go viral for the wrong reason.

I get asked all the time, 'Nick, how do you hold your tongue in that situation?' Chaos Controller is my secret weapon. It's my internal control tower when life drops chaos bombs unannounced, which is every effing day. And pause! You might not think it, but some of my best work has come from using this mega cheat code instead of detonating an emotionally dysregulated bomb. I've done those as well, and they never end well, even if it feels incredibly satisfying in the moment. That instant gratification soon ebbs away and you're left with the messy clean up.

Action

Now it's your turn to build your own cheat code combo.

Pick **one scenario** from your upcoming week where your usual ADHD spiral loves to show up. This could be:

- A morning where you need laser focus and memory support because you have to get something done, but there is too much noise in your head. Try Memory Index.
- A project which has been running smoothly has had to course correct, because a senior leader, who was asked for input a hundred times, has suddenly responded, and of course they have an opinion. You need Chaos Controller for this one and a takeaway for

dinner. Which will be you reward if you don't go on a rampage.

- A task that needs both vision and visibility. This could be your team plan for the year, budgeting, or your own performance objectives. The Colour Compass will be your North Star here.

Remember, this is a test drive. You will stumble, or you might smash it first time. Neither outcome means it will be the same next time. This is another set of tools to add to your what should now be an overflowing kit.

What's next?

I've given you the six superpowers, cheat codes, and strategies for pairing them up, but you don't need to do this alone, and you shouldn't. We all need a support system, and that looks different for everyone depending on their personal circumstance and where they are in their ADHD journey.

The next chapter shares how you can build a support system, suggestions for further learning, and how to look after yourself. Wellbeing is crucially important, and something we ADHDers will often forget. We're not doing that in this book.

Chapter 14

The Support System

Every comic book legend, every unstoppable force, every genius strategist has a team behind them. A mentor, a trusted guide, a group of people who remind them who they are when things get tough. No one wins battles without back-up, and no one masters their mind without support. This doesn't mean you need an entourage. A team can be two people, or two million. The point that I want to get across here is that you don't need to do this alone, and by this, I mean life, because ... life is hard.

Having ADHD, or any neurodivergent condition, can often feel like a solo mission, but it shouldn't be. Your brain doesn't operate in isolation, and neither should your personal growth. Whether it's friends who see your strengths when you forget them, colleagues who understand how you work, family who keep you grounded, or even a random internet stranger who says exactly what you need to hear at the right moment, support from others makes an enormous difference.

Support systems look different for everyone. Some people thrive with close-knit communities, while others operate better with a handful of select, trusted connections. Maybe you have a few go-to people who always have your back, or maybe your support system is built from different pockets of relationships that serve unique needs.

Mastering your ADHD superpowers isn't just about personal effort, it's about knowing who and what can help you along the way. ADHD doesn't always make things easy, and nobody is expected to navigate it alone. Have people to challenge you, remind you of your strengths, help when energy runs low and be there for the wins and setbacks.

Building a team of allies

Support systems look different for everyone, but one thing is universal: you need allies. Even if life has taken people away, or circumstances have made it harder to rely on others, there is always a way to build the connections that help you navigate challenges. I've experienced this firsthand, by losing both my parents at a young age, and I needed time by myself to grieve and process, but I still had support all around me, which I could rely on when I needed it. So, who could be your allies?

First, there's family, whether that means parents, siblings, extended relatives, or chosen family. These are the people who know you best, see you spiralling even when you don't, and support your growth by reminding you of how great you are. Family isn't always perfect, and sometimes the relationships are too damaged to rely on this group, but you can build your own family. It doesn't have to be blood relatives. Family is whatever you want to make it.

Next, there are friends, the ones who accept you exactly as you are. Friends are often the most adaptable part of a support system, stepping in when motivation fades, showing up when reassurance is needed, and helping you see progress when self-doubt creeps in. You can be more vulnerable in front of friends than you can with family. That's not the case for everyone, and childhood friends have a different dynamic, as there is a sense of duty and obligation, like with family. But the friends we choose as an adult are different, because we're on a level playing field. And if you're not, then you should ask yourself if that friendship is giving you any value.

Support can also come from colleagues. People you work alongside who respect your strengths, accommodate areas where you struggle and help you stay accountable in professional settings. The right colleagues understand how you function and offer encouragement instead of judgement. Not all colleagues become friends, and that's okay. You have a big part of your life in common for a defined period, and spend a lot of time with each other. That still doesn't mean the relationship isn't a valuable support system whilst you are working together. I've met some amazing people during my career, but now we no longer work together we've lost touch. It happens, and it's not a bad thing.

Next up are mentors. Someone who has been through similar experiences and offers guidance. Mentorship can be formal, structured and intentional, or it can be something that naturally grows. A conversation, a passing insight, a person whose words stay with you long after they're spoken. Sometimes, one sentence from the right person is enough to completely reframe how you approach your challenges. I've had mentors, and been a mentor and still do both. It can be formal or informal, but it's something which has not only helped me grow as a person, but I've witnessed the effect mentoring has had on hundreds of people during my career. If you don't currently have a mentor, get one.

Finally, we have strangers. These are people who unexpectedly provide exactly the support you needed, often without even realising it. This could be a social media post that speaks directly to your experience, a podcast episode that shifts your perspective, or a conversation with someone at the bus stop whose words stuck with you. Support doesn't always come from obvious places. Sometimes, it's hidden in small interactions that can change the way you approach your latest challenge.

Having allies means you don't have to carry everything alone. Building those connections makes ADHD feel less isolating, turning progress into a shared experience.

Professional support: If it's right for you

Some people thrive with self-guided strategies, figuring things out as they go. Others find professional support to be life-changing, offering structure, guidance, and resources that make everything feel more manageable. Neither approach is right or wrong. It's just about finding what works best for you.

Seeking professional help isn't about fixing something that's broken, it's about giving yourself access to tools that can make daily life smoother. For some, it means learning new techniques to regulate emotions. For others, it's about finding medical solutions that improve focus or clarity, and these are just two examples. I've used three different approaches over the years and will share these with you. This is not an exhaustive list and you need to find what works for you and speak to a medical professional.

I've seen the same therapist for over a decade. We first started working together during the year from hell I mentioned at the start of this book. Our relationship has grown over the years. What started as a short-term solution to support me through a grieving period became an immense source of support. As I went through various life events, my ADHD diagnosis and my recent autism diagnosis, my therapist was a constant. Sometimes I see her weekly, and other times it's monthly, but I always like to have an appointment in the diary. I regard it as my safe space where I can speak completely unfiltered with no judgement. Because I have to manage my emotions carefully every day, being in the corporate world, it helps to know I have someone I can vent to. Of course, I have people in my life I can do this with as well, but loved ones often feel the need to try and fix things for you. I am guilty of this as well. For me, my therapy sessions give me an outlet I need to handle whatever life wants to throw at me next.

I've tried medication in different forms over the years, and it rarely agrees with me. It's also difficult to get ADHD medication in the UK. It depends where you live and whether your doctor will prescribe it to you. I now take a small dose of an anti-anxiety medication, which helps me with emotional dysregulation. I've been prescribed a higher dose when I've been under intense stress, but my body doesn't react well to it. It's not something I intend to stay on forever but, for now, it helps take the edge off when things get challenging. I know fellow ADHDers who are on medication and it has been a lifesaver to them, but they get nothing out of therapy. There's no rule on what works best, so never listen to what anyone else says regarding medication unless they are a medical professional.

The third type of professional help I've had is coaching. This is a formal arrangement, which you may get your work to pay for or else fund it yourself. I'm an accredited coach, and have used a professional coach myself a few times over my career. It works differently to therapy. The two can complement each other or be completely separate. For me, having a coach who asks me challenging questions about the situations I'm dealing with at work has been invaluable. Whether the coaching is to help me navigate a challenging period, or give me focus on a specific goal, it is always meant to be short term. Whereas therapy can keep going, I would typically not work with a coach for longer than twelve months before taking a break.

There's no single roadmap for navigating ADHD, and there's no checklist you're required to follow. Your journey is yours, and professional support is just one option in your toolkit. Whatever you decide, the most important thing is that you're making choices that serve your wellbeing, growth and long-term success.

Never stop learning

If there's one constant in mastering your ADHD superpowers, it's that growth never stops. There's always another insight waiting, another technique to refine and another perspective that shifts the way you see things.

There are endless resources to help you. Books, podcasts, blogs, social media influencers. People sharing their lived experiences, breakthroughs, strategies and missteps. And while no single approach fits everyone, staying engaged with fresh ideas ensures you never get stuck in outdated methods that don't serve you any more.

I wanted to use this chapter to share some other self-development books, which have not only affected me personally and professionally, but influenced how I approached writing this book. When I thought about which books would be most effective for you in helping you master your superpowers, these were the ten which stood out to me. They are all five-star reads, so if you'd like further reading, check out some of these:

1. ***Mindset* by Carol Dweck:** If Mental Morph is your focus, this book is for you. It breaks down the difference between fixed and growth mindsets, showing how flexible thinking leads to long-term success.
2. ***Atomic Habits* by James Clear:** The perfect book for reinforcing Mind Vault and Impulse Shield. It dives into how small daily changes compound into massive results, creating a structure for habit-building that actually works.
3. ***Essentialism* by Greg McKeown:** Feeling scattered or overwhelmed? This book helps with prioritisation, ensuring attention and energy go toward what truly matters.

4. ***The Smart but Scattered Guide to Success* by Peg Dawson and Richard Guare:** A book which focuses on ADHD executive function mastery, covering strategies for organisation, productivity and self-regulation. This is focused on adult ADHD.
5. ***The 7 Habits of Highly Effective People* by Stephen R. Covey:** If you're looking for a roadmap to personal and professional effectiveness, this book is packed with wisdom on discipline, planning and mindset shifts. A good one if you're looking to develop Vision Crafter.
6. ***Deep Work* by Cal Newport:** This book explores how to eliminate distractions, train the mind for deep concentration and create a lasting impact with intentional work habits. The perfect combination for the power of Focus Beam.
7. ***Eat That Frog!* by Brian Tracy:** If procrastination is the enemy, this book helps with task execution, tackling priorities and overcoming mental resistance. This is a book I give out to graduates in their first week. It's perfect for those who struggle with time management.
8. ***Emotional Intelligence* by Daniel Goleman:** A perfect fit for Impulse Shield, offering insights into emotional awareness, regulation and communication mastery.

Goleman is considered the godfather of emotional intelligence, as it was his book which popularised the subject. Definitely worth a read, especially if you'd like to understand the science behind EQ.

9. ***Stuffocation* by James Walkman:** If mental clutter is causing chaos, this book explores the power of minimalism, not just in physical space, but in mental clarity. A good one for the Mind Vault superpower, and for those who work in chaotic spaces.
10. ***Grit* by Angela Duckworth:** Mental Morph and resilience go hand in hand, and this book dives deep into perseverance, determination and the mindset required for long-term success. If you struggle with resilience, this book is well worth a read.

Managing burnout before it manages you

ADHD brains don't come with an off switch. They operate at full speed until they hit a wall, which means the cycle is often go, go, go, and then crash. I shared one of my crashes in my origin story, but there have been others, and I know there will be more before I shuffle off this Earth. However, there would have been a lot more crashes in my life were it not for me utilising my superpowers. But you need to do more than that. You need to look after yourself and not assume somebody is going to do it for you, which is kind of an ironic thing to say after I just spoke about the importance of allies. But ADHDers are classic rescuers, and will rush to help someone else to our own detriment. We are wired for constant stimulation, making it easy to ignore exhaustion until it forces a complete shutdown. It's important you don't forget to look after yourself.

One of the most effective tools for preventing ADHD burnout is scheduled downtime. Rest shouldn't just happen when exhaustion wins. It needs to be built into your routine, deliberately and consistently. Waiting until you're too tired to function means recovery takes longer and feels overwhelming.

I aim to schedule a week off work every three months. Rather than have a long holiday in the summer, I would rather have shorter ones. I don't always go away for those weeks off, but I make a point of relaxing, even if it's laying on the couch in my office and reading a dozen books, going to a local spa or doing a bit of life admin which doesn't require any thinking. The downtime is important to me. I know my body, and twelve weeks is my threshold for when I need to take a breather.

It's not just the long breaks, but those small breaks throughout the day and week. Solo time matters, even for extroverts. Being around people constantly can feel energising for some, but mentally draining for others. ADHD brains process interactions at high speed, meaning enjoyable conversations are still exhausting. Finding quiet reset moments, whether it's alone in a room, taking a walk or simply stepping away from the noise for a few minutes, ensures burnout doesn't sneak up unexpectedly. I would consider myself mostly extrovert, and work in HR, but even I have said, 'I'm all peopled out!' on many an occasion.

Action

No one thrives alone, and the strongest superheroes know when to lean on their allies, invest in their wellbeing and keep learning. To build and refine your support system, try this three-step action plan:

1. **Assess your current support system:** Take a moment to identify the people, professionals and resources that actively support your growth and wellbeing. You might be surprised when you write it down.
2. **Integrate intentional downtime into your routine:** ADHD doesn't believe in slowing down until it crashes, so build structured downtime before burnout hits. Test different recovery techniques. Some people need a week off every three months, others need a long weekend every month and there are many variations in between.
3. **Commit to ongoing learning:** Pick one book, blog or podcast to explore. It doesn't need to be on the list I have provided here, but pick something else you are going to read or listen

to in the next two weeks which supports your personal development goals.

Your progress isn't about perfection, it's about momentum. Having a strong support system ensures you keep moving forward without burning out along the way.

What's next?

Our time together is shortly ending as we only have one chapter left. Then, it's over to you to take what you need from this book and implement it. My work here will be done, but before I say goodbye, we have one last hurrah.

Chapter 15

The Beginning

I feel a weird sense of déjà vu, because I'm back in the coffee shop, with a latte and sausage bap, yet it's been eight weeks since I wrote the first line of this book. I have no idea when it will be published, because my editor needs to comb through my ramblings first and make sense of everything. By the time you read this, it should all make sense. It is now July 12, 2025, and I'm determined this book will be in people's hands before the year is out.

I've called the final chapter 'The Beginning' for a reason. This is where your superhero origin story starts. Understanding your executive functions and developing your superpowers isn't a quick fix. There's no finish line, ultimate mastery or perfect path where progress moves forward without setbacks.

Learning to navigate ADHD is a journey that you'll be on for the rest of your life, and I'm not saying that to convey a sense of doom and gloom. Neurotypical people don't have everything figured out either. We have no way of knowing what the world will look like in ten years, let alone fifty. Our brains don't know what they don't know.

I don't claim to be perfect, or a master of my ADHD superpowers, but I didn't have the easiest start in life, and have clawed my way to the top of my chosen career ladder. I put that down to understanding how I can use **my strengths** to achieve **my goals**, rather than being stopped by other people's view on what's wrong with me, or struggle to achieve what is effectively somebody else's goal. That's an important thing to remember. You only get one life, and you should not be living it for someone else. Your life. Your dreams.

Mastering your superpowers isn't about perfection. It's about awareness. Knowing your strengths, understanding your barriers and finding practical strategies that work for you. No one expects you to wake up tomorrow with flawless productivity, effortless memory recall and an unshakable ability to resist distractions, because I hate to break this to you, but that is not happening. The goal of this book isn't to turn you into someone else, it's helping you refine the skills that allow you to become the best version of yourself you can be, and reach your full potential. Not everybody will be a CEO, nor does everybody want to. Hats off to anyone who wants the stress of that job. As I said before, your dream is for you, just as your superhero journey will be.

If there's one takeaway from this book, it's this: you are not broken. You are not failing. You are not behind. ADHD doesn't make success impossible, it just requires a different approach, one tailored to how your brain operates, not how others expect it to function, whether that be a manager, family member or society. There is nothing wrong with being different. If people have a problem, then it's their problem. I think you're awesome, especially as you've got past all my ramblings to the end of this book. Who says you can't focus?

But now, the actual work begins. Not in trying to fix yourself, but in building on everything you've learned, testing the cheat codes, adjusting when things don't work and giving yourself the space to grow at your own pace. There will be moments when it feels frustrating, when progress seems slow and when you surprise yourself with how much you've grown. And through all of it, remember, you don't owe anybody anything. This is your superhero origin story, and those doubters and pessimists can politely bugger off.

To wrap things up, I'm going to provide you with a brief recap of the six superpowers and cheat codes. This will make it easy to refer to when that working memory is having an off day, so you know which chapter to jump to.

Your superpowers and how to keep growing

Designed to enhance the six executive functions of the brain, these superpowers both turbo-charge your strengths and give you strategies to overcome your barriers. My advice is don't do everything at once, and only focus on two superpowers. One which is holding you back, and another which people call you out on as a strength. That latter is your USP. It's what makes you stand out at work, home or anywhere you want. So, why not make it even stronger? That's my advice, but as I've said, this is your story.

Focus Beam

This is not just about being able to hyper-focus on something you are passionate about. Most ADHD brains can do that. This is about being able to control it. Need to hyper-focus on something that is mind-numbingly boring, such as an audit report? Sorry, again, auditors! Focus Beam gives you the power to turn it on when you need to. The last time, I'll make that joke, well in this book! Focus Beam also gives you the power to not go too far down the rabbit hole when you are in the zone, and are possibly going in the wrong direction.

Vision Crafter

Designed to combat planning and organisation procrastination. Ideas are great but, without structure, they turn into mental clutter, which makes no sense to anyone, even you. Vision Crafter brings your 'vision' to life. I know, but that was too easy. This superpower isn't about rigid schedules, it's about creating adaptable frameworks that guide progress while allowing flexibility. We ADHDers need to know where we are going, but we also want to stop and look at shiny things on the way. Vision Crafter gives you the skills to do that.

Time Warp

Time management is something everybody struggles with at some point, but ask yourself if it's time management or prioritising, as you might be in the wrong superpower. ADHD brains often misinterpret time, leading to deadlines sneaking up like an ambush or tasks stretching far beyond what was planned. Mastering Time Warp means developing an awareness of time perception, using structured techniques to track, manage and optimise how you allocate it. There will be no more missed deadlines with this superpower, he says, still writing when this book is due with my editor in two days.

Mind Vault

Holding onto important details isn't just about remembering facts, it's about creating a reliable mental storage system. My phone is right next to me. You will be pleased to know I haven't lost it at all today. How amazing is that? I will reward myself with a lemon muffin later if I get this chapter done. Where was I? Ah, yes, Mind Vault. This superpower ensures key information stays accessible when you need it, improving your ability to recall tasks, conversations and essential knowledge without the daily struggle or that constant look of bewilderment on your face.

Mental Morph

Change is inevitable, and Mental Morph ensures you don't just survive it, you thrive in it. We are now in a world where 'steady as she goes' no longer exists, so this is a trying time for our ADHD brains. This superpower helps you shift smoothly, absorb new information, alter perspectives and embrace unfamiliar situations without panic. Strengthening this skill ensures that uncertainty becomes an opportunity, not an obstacle. Something we all could do with working on, ADHD brain or not.

Impulse Shield

My nemesis. Although, so far, this week has been fairly pleasant. I've only wanted to go on a rampage three times, so I'll take that as progress. Self-regulation isn't about suppressing impulses, and I will keep banging that drum. It's about controlling them before they cause chaos. Impulse Shield ensures you pause before acting, filter emotional responses and choose thoughtful action over instinctive reaction.

Your ADHD Toolkit

These cheat codes will serve you well in life. Tinker around with them. Tweak them to your unique brain and find what works best for you. I would love to hear how you get on.

Here is a quick recap of the six cheat codes:

- **DOPE Engine:** Activates hyper-focus through the perfect set-up. Distractions off, environment prepped, preferences dialled in and a clear reward at the finish line. This is about being in control of when you consciously move to hyper-focus.
- **Colour Codex:** Your visual workflow filter. The last time I mention Post-its, I promise. Pink for priority, Orange for order, Green for go and Blue for buffer.
- **Element Compass:** Helps you understand your brain's operating style - Wind, Fire, Rain or Earth - so you can work with your energy, not against it. You could be a mix of two, so listen to what your body and brain are saying each day, and use your element to your advantage.
- **ECHO Index:** Locks in memory through emotion, rhythm, repetition and smart organisation. This means the important stuff sticks and shows up when you need it, and you always know where your phone is.
- **FLIP Circuit:** Guides you through change calmly and with strategy. Feel it, let it go, adapt, then pivot like you planned it all along. Change is inevitable, and we need to get better at developing our resilience. This cheat code will help you achieve that.

- **Silent SCREAM:** Your internal impulse control system, intercepting reactions, processing emotions and turning chaos into measured, intentional response. If I am going to use the term 'game changer' one last time, it would be here. This cheat code can completely transform your life.

If you'd like a free download of all the cheat codes, head over to my website – www.superpowermastery.com/free-book – and join my Superpower Squad and get my latest tips and tricks. I don't do spammy emails because I find them irritating myself, and would never remember to send something with excessive frequency.

Your next move

There is no action for you to do at the end of this chapter, because you've had enough peppered throughout. All I ask is that you don't put this book away and do nothing. Choose what you do next, carefully and tactically.

ADHD brains thrive on momentum, but struggle with overwhelm. Taking on every superpower at the same time will burn you out faster than it will improve your skills. I know I've said this before, but I am saying it again, because I know you better than you think you do. You have thought about doing them all, haven't you? Pick no more than two superpowers to develop, test the effectiveness of the cheat codes in your environment and let progress build naturally.

Look at your support system and decide on whether that is something you need to prioritise first. Go shopping for a shiny new notebook, and try not to buy out the stock. All I ask is that you commit to doing something regarding at least one superpower in the next month. Do it now. Tell yourself in your head. I'll wait ...

Wasn't so difficult, was it? Now, hold yourself to account, or share it with someone else if you need help with that and you are comfortable with that openness. I encourage it, but it's not for everyone.

I wish you every success in what you do next. Everyone can be brilliant, including you. Don't compare yourself to others, not even other ADHDers. Have your own goals and dreams, and I hope something from this book will give you a helping hand in achieving them. But, at the end of it all, the only one who can turn you into an ADHD superhero is yourself, so good luck and have fun doing it!

Before you go back to the chaos

Need more support?

If this book lit a spark, there's so much more waiting for you.

As a result of writing this book, I founded **Superpower Mastery**, a training, coaching and mentoring business which builds neuro-inclusive superpower frameworks to enable people to unlock their brilliance and reach their full potential. Whether that's the ADHD superpowers you learned in this book, or others which can you support you in the workplace, be that leadership, or career superpowers. There is something for everyone.

Join the Superhero Squad

Sign up at www.superpowermastery.com/free-book to grab your free ADHD superpower cheat code handbook, which gives you all the cheat codes from this book in a quick and easy format.

Explore digital learning

You'll find ADHD-friendly learning materials designed to support your development journey in mastering your ADHD superpowers. These are in the Superpower Academy section of my website which is growing all the time.

Want to go further?

If you're ready for deeper transformation, I offer coaching and mentoring support tailored to your goals, your pace, and your superpowers. Whether it's leadership, career growth, or just figuring out how to stop losing your phone, I'd be honoured to help you. You can contact me via my website.

One final word from me

You're not too much. You're not too messy. You're exactly what the world needs.

Acknowledgments

To Richard, Rhodri, and Emily: thank you for your sharp eyes, steady hands, and creative brilliance. This book wouldn't be here if it wasn't for your editing, proofing and design skills.

To my husband: thank you for letting me be my authentic, chaotic, unfiltered self... not that you had much choice in the matter.

To every colleague, collaborator, and character I've worked with over the past 20 years, whether you lifted me up or taught me the hard way, you helped shape the superpowers I now wear with pride.

To my therapist: thank you for keeping me (mostly) sane for over a decade. You deserve a medal, or at least a quiet holiday.

To my fellow ADHDers: you are the heartbeat of this book. Your brilliance, resilience, and refusal to dim your light inspire me daily. Never stop being your brilliant selves.

www.ingramcontent.com/pod-product-compliance
Lightning Source LLC
LaVergne TN
LVHW052313200926
848481LV00002B/551

PHARMACOLOGY - RESEARCH, SAFETY TESTING AND REGULATION

AMOXICILLIN

MEDICAL USES, MECHANISM OF ACTION AND POTENTIAL ADVERSE EFFECTS

Pharmacology - Research, Safety Testing and Regulation